KU-611-395

# On training to be a therapist
## The long and winding road to qualification

**John Karter**

**Open University Press**

Open University Press
McGraw-Hill Education
McGraw-Hill House
Shoppenhangers Road
Maidenhead
Berkshire
England
SL6 2QL

email: enquiries@openup.co.uk
world wide web: www.openup.co.uk

and

Two Penn Plaza, New York, NY 10121–2289, USA

First Published 2002
Reprinted 2008 (twice), 2010

Copyright © John Karter 2002

All rights reserved. Except for the quotation of short passages for the purpose of criticism and review, no part of this publication may be reproduced, stored in a retrieval system, or transmitted, in any form or by any means, electronic, mechanical, photocopying, recording or otherwise, without the prior written permission of the publisher or a licence from the Copyright Licensing Agency Limited. Details of such licences (for reprographic reproduction) may be obtained from the Copyright Licensing Agency Ltd of 90 Tottenham Court Road, London, W1P 0LP.

A catalogue record of this book is available from the British Library

ISBN-10 0 335 21001 5 (pb)   0 335 21002 3 (hb)
ISBN-13 978 0 335 21001 5 (pb)     978 0 335 21002 2 (hb)

*Library of Congress Cataloging-in-Publication Data*
Karter, John, 1945–
    On training to be a therapist: the long and winding road to qualification/
John Karter.
      p. cm.
    Includes bibliographical references and index.
    ISBN 0-335-21002-3 (hb) – ISBN 0-335-21101-5 (pbk.)
    1. Psychotherapists–Training of.   2. Psychotherapists–Certification.
    3. Psychotherapy–Study and teaching.   I. Title.

RC459. K37 2002
616.89′14′0711–dc21

                                                                2002023854

Typeset by Graphicraft Limited, Hong Kong
Printed in Great Britain by CPI Antony Rowe, Chippenham, Wiltshire

*To the 'Tuesday Psychos' – fabulous friends who made training a very special experience.*

# Contents

# Acknowledgements

I would like to express my sincere thanks to the staff and students of Metanoia Institute, Regent's College School of Psychotherapy and Counselling, and Westminster Pastoral Foundation, as well as students past and present from many other sources, for their cooperation and help in completing my student questionnaires. This book would not have been possible without their invaluable contributions. Many thanks, in addition, to all other tutors and supervisors who contributed material. I am also immeasurably grateful to Linda Nissim, Dr Freddie Strasser and Dr Adrienne Baker for reading the manuscript and offering helpful and insightful comments and suggestions which greatly enhanced the finished product, and to Penny Martin for researching material for the book.

# Foreword

Amongst the many helpful pieces of advice given to John Karter, or passed on by him from his own experience of training as a therapist, was one about books: 'Books are just one element of your training. Don't try to understand everything you read. Pick out the bits that seem relevant to you' (p. 66).

Sound advice, as much else is in this book. But it left me wondering whether, with all those other books to dip into in training, one on training itself would get a look-in. There are a number of good reasons why it should.

This is one book that *will* be easy to understand. Karter's journalistic experience makes for a smooth read, a successful blend of anecdote and thoughtful commentary upon the very books and authors whom it is indeed sometimes difficult to understand.

Karter's brush is a broad one. His own training, building upon a psychodynamic towards an integrative approach is clear from the many different sources he cites in support of his guide to students – it's a book for anyone on any course, whatever the orientation.

It's not a 'how-to' book, of which there are already too many; it's what we used to call a 'vade mecum' – a companion along the way; a book the reader will want to dip into; one that falls somewhere between reading therapeutic literature, and that other literature which students should be encouraged to read, as Karter himself suggests, which is nothing to do with therapy. Of course this book is about therapy, but it takes a healthy step or two back from the intensive world of training, and helps students (and indeed trainers) to see things in perspective.

Above all, before the reader gets into those long reading lists which courses have to hand out, perhaps even before the reader starts applying for courses at all, this is a book not just to dip into, but read from cover to cover. I don't imagine that what Karter has to say, from his own and fellow students' experience, will put the serious applicant off, because he does not paint a pessimistic picture. But he does describe much of the reality of what training is like, with its satisfactions as well as its frustrations, and prepares the reader for what probably is to come.

Finally, trainers will also find this a helpful reminder of what perhaps was their own experience, long since suppressed, but sometimes meted out on unsuspecting students as 'this is what I had to go through, so you must expect to do the same' – although this is sometimes more, as goal-posts change and professional standards demand more and more of trainers and students alike. The experiences described in this book, and the careful reflection on them, may even provoke a debate about whether some of what we put our trainees through is really necessary!

*Michael Jacobs*

# Introduction

I have often thought that training to be a psychotherapist or counsellor is not unlike learning to drive a car. You know how it is in those first few frenetic driving lessons; you feel you simply do not have enough hands to do everything – grip the steering wheel, change gear, adjust the mirror, honk the horn, signal, and carry out the hundred and one other tasks demanded of you by your driving teacher, the Highway Code and the idiosyncrasies of the car itself. The actual business of driving along the road to your destination is almost entirely forgotten in the midst of all the cack-handed manoeuvering, theorizing and frantic attempts to remain in control.

Therapy training can often appear to involve the same delicate – and often seemingly impossible – feat of all-encompassing dexterity. The never-ending round of theory, essay writing, clinical work, supervision and personal therapy is difficult enough, and when students are simultaneously juggling these with a job, a family and the incessant demands of life itself, it is easy to feel overwhelmed, alone, unsupported and despondent – to name just a few of the negative emotions that can assert themselves during training (as I will highlight, there can be many positive emotions, too).

The sense of being gradually and inexorably submerged to a point where it appears impossible to clamber back to terra firma can reach a nadir when you are faced with the harsh reality of blending together all those disparate elements of training in your first sessions with clients, in stark contrast to the cosseted theorizing of the lecture room or the cocoon of those comfy role plays with fellow students. When Wilfrid Bion (1974: 13) made his famous statement 'In every consulting room there ought to be two rather frightened people, the patient and the psychoanalyst' he was clearly not thinking of trainees. Many of those who are still wrestling with their L-plates are not merely frightened – they are gradually drowning in an ever-broadening sea of confusion and self-doubt.

As the patient sits there pouring his heart out in the hope of insight and deliverance, everything comes at you so fast it is easy to feel that you could use not so much an extra pair of hands as half a dozen extra frontal lobes. Sundry bits of Freud, Winnicott, Klein or whichever theorist you have been trying to assimilate, surge into your consciousness, only to be pushed aside by the amazingly astute observations your supervisor came out with at the last supervision session, or the unfathomable clinical precepts your tutor heaped upon you in last week's lecture.

If I appear to be indulging in a degree of hyperbole, it is simply to make a point, the essence of which can be said to underpin the basic rationale for this book. The process involved in qualifying to be a therapist is unlike any other training in the demands it makes on us as people. Not only can the experience engender self-doubt, isolation and varying levels of stress, it also involves the individual in a relentless exercise in self-reflection and self-examination, often leading to seminal changes as a person, which in turn can destabilize relationships with family and friends, sometimes beyond repair, and can thus fundamentally alter the trainee's whole way of being in the world.

Many trainees suffer in silence as they wrestle with their particular training demons. Simply getting through it sometimes seems the only way, with much of the mental energy and psychic creativity that should have been directed towards the careful nurturing of the evolving therapist being channelled instead into an extended exercise in damage limitation. As essays pile up, patients present increasingly unfathomable material, and supervisors tear case presentations to shreds, it is all to easy to indulge in an orgy of self-condemnation and to slink away, licking self-inflicted wounds, to consider why on earth you ever considered training in the first place.

The syndrome of self-questioning can have a malignant quality about it: self-doubt spirals into persecutory anxiety, which in turn obliterates all sense of perspective. So, for example, if a patient fails to show, especially in the early stages of training, it is difficult to believe that the non-appearance may be due to resistance, acting out or even a genuine reason for being unable to attend the session. It can only be the result of your inept and woefully-clumsy handling of the previous session,

# Introduction

your crass interventions, your total failure to empathize and personal qualities that clearly make you more suited to being a tax inspector.

Feeling constantly judged by tutors (which, of course, is an undeniable reality) and comparing oneself unfavourably to one's peers can heighten negative feelings. Personal therapy can help but, in the early stages at least the process of therapy can feel more deconstructive than therapeutic and it, too, often has to be shoehorned in to an already bulging schedule. So, what should be a benign and supportive component of training courses can often be viewed as just another element of the overall pressure cooker situation rather than a release valve.

As the journey unfolds, it is easy to feel very alone and to develop a sense of lacking any real support network, with nowhere to offload one's burdens and concerns. There is the occasional tutorial where students can discuss their progress in terms of the course itself, but, on most trainings, the reality is that the facility for attending to personal needs is woefully inadequate and has simply not been built into the system. A feeling of alienation can begin to arise and this can be compounded by a burgeoning sense of distance from partners and family, who not only find it difficult to comprehend this bizarre undertaking in which we have become so irretrievably embroiled, but often feel seriously threatened by it as well.

I vividly recall my own personal crisis, which arrived with devastating suddenness during the early part of my first diploma in psychodynamic counselling and psychotherapy. Having become utterly dispirited by what I perceived as the vastly superior knowledge and experience of my fellow students, and feeling weighed down by a reading list that seemed to encompass the entire global library of psychotherapeutic literature, I decided the whole thing was a ghastly mistake and resolved to scurry back to the safety of my former life as a journalist.

Fortunately, I was rescued by the timely intervention of my course leader, who, on hearing of my decision to quit, called me in for a talk and subtly guided me back on track again. In pointing out that I had become enmeshed in a classic scenario of what Kleinians term 'splitting', she enabled me to see that because of my fears and insecurity I had subconsciously painted myself into a corner by setting up a situation of perceived extremes, denigrating my new life as a trainee therapist whilst idealizing the old one as an established journalist.

Several years further down the line, I am still immeasurably grateful to this insightful woman for preventing me from making what would have been one of the worst mistakes of my life due to feelings of being unable to cope and a lack of self-belief. To a certain extent, these feelings were there before I signed up for the course, but they were swelled to untenable proportions by the pressures of training.

# On training to be a therapist

Having flagged up some of the potentially negative aspects of training, it is important to state here and now that it is certainly not my aim to frighten off prospective trainees, nor to dampen the enthusiasm of those already in training – quite the contrary. Besides the benefits of learning and developing on a professional level, therapy training can offer profound, life-changing experiences that are often wholly positive and self-enhancing. In my own case, after negotiating that early crisis, I was able to enjoy the training in all its fullness, forming wonderful, lasting friendships with like-minded people and opening myself up to a whole range of new attitudes, beliefs and ways of being. This kind of openness is, I believe, an essential ingredient in maximizing both the personal and professional elements of training.

Having stayed on to train for six years in all, I became fascinated by the nature and rationale of the heterogeneous process of therapy training, especially the diverse and very profound effects on students. It gradually began to dawn on me that something fundamental and vital had been allowed to go missing by default. Observing fellow students wrestling with academic, clinical and personal issues, I realized that the 'X-factor' that so often became lost in this melange of constant pressure and self-analysis was any sense of genuine enjoyment of the course *per se*, or of finding fulfilment and meaning in the process of training itself.

To look at it in therapeutic terms, I am referring to the ability to play in the Winnicottian sense. Winnicott (1999: 54) suggested that playing leads to creativity and a search for the self. In putting forward his theory of playing, he wrote (1999: 38):

> *Psychotherapy takes place in the overlap of two areas of playing, that of the patient and that of the therapist. Psychotherapy has to do with two people playing together. The corollary of this is that where playing is not possible then the work done by the therapist is directed towards bringing the patient from a state of not being able to play into a state of being able to play.*

I would venture to suggest that it would be possible, even desirable, to extend Winnicott's idea of playing to therapy training, substituting the relationship of therapist–patient with tutor–trainee. If we carry on this theme, Winnicott's idea of 'potential space' would also be apposite. In stating that play starts in the baby's move away from its mother, Winnicott says: 'The playground is a potential space between the mother and the baby or joining mother and baby' (1999: 47). In the case of training, the potential space would be the course itself, where the student can learn how to play and be creative on his way to his individuation as a therapist.

4

# Introduction

I would take my X-factor concept a stage further and suggest that trainees should be encouraged to foster a capacity for humour and a concomitant sense of fun. That might seem to some to be a questionable requirement for a process that is steeped in (or perhaps that should be weighed down by) gravitas, and no doubt those who find it difficult to justify taking it anything less than 100 per cent earnestly will be ruthlessly querying and analysing my need to 'lighten up'. However, it is my firm belief that a little levity, and even a measure of irreverence, is all too often conspicuous by its absence.

The inherent contradictions and absurdities of life, and, from an existential point of view, its ultimate meaninglessness, could seem unbearable if we did not have the capacity to bring a counterbalancing sense of irony or even whimsicality to the more tragic and hopeless aspects of the human condition (always being careful to maintain the respect and care which should be fundamental in our dealings with our clients). Such an attitude goes hand in glove with the need to question established wisdom in psychotherapy and counselling, which, I believe, can only be regarded as a good thing in the context of the eternal quest for a deeper understanding of the complex and often unfathomable workings of the human psyche.

When I talk of a need for levity, I am not suggesting that we stop taking our training seriously and appear in lectures wearing party hats and red noses, or ask our patients if they have heard the one about the English, Irish and Scottish psychotherapists. However, developing a capacity for seeing the lighter side or the more paradoxical nature of certain situations can make training less onerous and more creative, and ultimately, I believe, it can make us better therapists.

The notion of this missing X-factor fired my imagination and led me to begin writing a monthly column entitled 'On Being In Training' for *The Psychotherapy Review* (now sadly defunct). Whilst I was keen to ensure that the column looked at the various training issues mentioned above from a serious point of view, because it seemed essential to offer student readers something they could take away and utilize, I was equally intent on taking a deliberately lighter, more user-friendly stance towards the issues that mattered to trainees.

The idea was to enable, or perhaps empower, students to regain not only a sense of perspective but also, to paraphrase the title of Milan Kundera's celebrated novel, to introduce a more bearable lightness of being to their lives as trainees. I was both touched and heartened by responses from fellow students on my own and other courses who told me they welcomed the column because there was a huge need to address these issues in an accessible and 'real' way. It was suggested by one or two kind souls that there might even be a book to be written on

# On training to be a therapist

the subject – and so the idea of 'On Training to be a Therapist' was conceived.

Before approaching a publisher I needed at least to do some minimal research into a target market and thus a rationale for the book. My sense was that there were not just battalions but whole armies of students out there, many of whom would be struggling with exactly the kind of issues with which I proposed to deal. My initial enquiries certainly confirmed this, in numerical terms at least. I discovered, for example, that the British Association for Counselling and Psychotherapy lists 500 training courses in its directory, and receives annually 5000 phone calls, 2000 letters and 10,000 hits on their website from people enquiring about training. There are other umbrella training organizations, such as the United Kingdom Council for Psychotherapy, as well as a myriad of training institutions, who tell a similar story of a profession that is mushrooming at an extraordinary rate.

Furthermore, the responses to my student questionnaires – some sent out to major training institutions, some accessed in other ways – indicated that students felt many of these issues were simply not being addressed and that they often felt resentful that they were having to shoulder emotional burdens arising from training on their own. Talking to a number of them individually, it was clear that they were crying out for some kind of forum for discussion centred around the needs of trainees and/or a support network geared to looking at the personal and professional concerns and difficulties that students regularly encounter during training, rather than purely focusing on the shortcomings or parameters of the course itself, as most staff–student meetings tend to do. Also – at the risk of over-emphasizing my own project – many felt that the idea of some kind of 'experiential guidebook' devoted to this whole area and written from an insider's viewpoint would be a real asset.

Thinking back to my previous incarnation as a journalist, I remember when I joined *The Independent* newspaper on its inception in 1986, being summoned by the editor, Andreas Whittam Smith, to a gathering of all the journalistic staff before the first edition hit the streets. At this meeting he gave us a little pep talk based on the innovative direction in which he felt the paper should be pointed. One of the things he stressed was that the journalists should not do what many writers on other papers did, namely to write exclusively for fellow journalists in a way that aimed to impress and outdo their colleagues in the profession, and took no account of what the newspaper's most valuable asset, their readers, really wanted.

Sad to say, and without wishing to denigrate the many brilliant writers in the field of psychotherapy and counselling who are

# Introduction

the exception, it seems to me that there are far too many books in this field designed to do exactly what Whittam Smith sought to avoid. Thus, in writing this book, I have been keen to avoid falling into the trap of compiling just another academic book, top-heavy with abstruse theory and intellectual jousting, the kind of work that talks *at* students rather than *to* them. Having written the 'On Being In Training' columns when I was a student and begun this book when I was in the final term of my Advanced Diploma in Integrative Psychotherapy, I hope I have managed to engender and to maintain a 'one of us' feel to the writing (in one sense I believe we never relinquish our L-plates anyway).

I am well aware that my approach, especially when I examine certain theoretical and clinical issues, could leave me open to a charge of shallowness, but in this context I must stress that it was never my intention to provide a full and complete analysis of the areas of theory and practice which are touched on within these pages. There are already more than enough books looking at these matters from every conceivable angle, and to have even attempted to emulate or recycle them would have defeated the whole object of the project.

What I have sought to do is to address the issues, whether clinical or otherwise, primarily from an experiential standpoint. If you like, I have offered a 'students' eye view', incorporating feedback from trainees of many different orientations (and also from qualified therapists), which provides a mixture of supportive and practical material. Thus Chapter 1 looks, *inter alia*, at the whole area of self-doubt and feelings of deconstruction, and the desirability of examining the reasons why we undertake training in the first place. Chapter 2 focuses on self-exploration and the effects that personal changes can have on ourselves and our relationships. Chapter 3 highlights the stresses and strains of training and how to survive them, and also covers two questions that are fundamental to working in the profession: 'What is it that we are seeking to achieve as therapists?' and 'Do we believe therapy works?'

Chapter 4 looks at the dangers of being too reliant on theory and adhering too strictly to any one clinical approach, and also deals with writing essays and case studies, a common area of difficulty for many students. Chapter 5 is dedicated to strategies and insights that can enable students to get the most from supervision, whilst Chapter 6 addresses feelings of inadequacy and 'stuckness' within the consulting room and examines the widespread – but usually misplaced – fear of making what are felt to be 'catastrophic' errors. Chapter 7 focuses on four major problem areas for students: unplanned contact with clients, direct questions from clients and whether to self-reveal, difficulties in working with transference or 'bringing it into the room', and feelings of sexuality in the consulting room. Chapter 8 looks at ending training and the mixed emotions this can engender, and also offers some practical suggestions for seeking work.

To summarize, what I have sought to produce is a kind of 'good companion' for what can seem like a long and often friendless journey, providing guidelines and hints on how to make the travelling more manageable, gratifying and liberating. The end result of training, professional qualification, cannot and should not be downplayed, but in chasing remorselessly after that little bit of paper it is easy to forego the opportunity to savour a unique experience. To that end, perhaps we should remember the words of Robert Louis Stevenson: 'To travel hopefully is a better thing than to arrive'.

\* \* \*

It seemed necessary before moving into the main text of the book to say something about my personal approach to therapy. My initial training was psychodynamic. However, whilst I very much valued that way of thinking, I found adhering to one model too narrow and constricting. Clients do not fit into tidy packages, as some theoreticians and clinicians would like us to believe. One needs to be able to adapt one's way of working to the individual. My advanced training was based on an integrative approach, which incorporated humanistic, existential and communicative thinking as well as psychodynamic. This enabled me to be open to a greater range of ideas and attitudes, and I now include some cognitive behavioural elements in my practice as well.

When people ask me what I consider my approach to be, I usually say 'integrative with a psychodynamic base' because the psychodynamic model still underpins my thinking to a great extent. This will become obvious from the way I address many of the theoretical and clinical concepts. However, I want to make it clear that I do not believe there is any ultimate truth or definitive way of working. There will be many readers whose models of theory and practice differ greatly from my own, but hopefully this will not detract from the overall concept of the book.

It also seemed appropriate to say just a few words on what might be termed technical matters. There has been much debate about whether there is any difference in essence between psychotherapy and counselling and it is neither necessary nor desirable to go into that here. My use of the term 'therapist' throughout, rather than 'psychotherapist' or 'counsellor', was not so much an avoidance of the issue as a matter of expediency and consistency. Suffice it to say that, in my opinion, the issues dealt with in the book apply equally to both trainee psychotherapists and trainee counsellors. As to the title, 'On Training to be a Psychotherapist

## Introduction

or Counsellor' seemed far too unwieldy, and therefore I again settled for the term 'Therapist', which covers both.

Whether to use the term 'client' or 'patient' seemed less clear cut. Once again there is much disagreement within the profession as to the precise meanings and implications attached to these labels, especially the word 'patient', which is often associated with the more psychologically disturbed type of individual usually seen in a hospital setting. Both terms will jar with some readers for various reasons, and in choosing to use the term 'client' in most instances throughout the book, I hope I will not be accused of fudging the issue. My reasoning was again linked to consistency and also to the fact that whereas counsellors almost exclusively favour the term 'client', psychotherapists use both terms.

# 1 Facing up to mission impossible

'Courage mounteth with occasion', William Shakespeare wrote in *King John*, highlighting the well-established phenomenon that human beings when faced with the threat of clear and present danger are often able to reach inside themselves to access hitherto unrecognized and untapped sources of bravery and resilience. In contrast to this notion and no less fascinating, is the manner in which we are prone to respond when confronted with the possibility of becoming overwhelmed by emotionally painful or humiliating circumstances and events, grasping at the merest scintilla of hope, however tenuous or bizarre this apparent means of deliverance may seem in more objective terms.

I remember experiencing something of this 'clutching at straws' syndrome when I attended an interview for a course in counselling several years ago. Arriving at the institute in question about half an hour early, my nerves jangling like a badly-tuned guitar, I noticed what struck me as a rather pathetic figure entering through the main gate just a few yards ahead of me. The individual in question was dressed in a shabby mac that would have shamed television's shoddiest detective, Colombo, and was clutching a beaten-up carrier bag.

He wore a battered pair of spectacles with one of the side-pieces broken off, which were secured around his neck by a dangling piece of what looked like old pyjama cord. His trousers, to use an expression often applied to schoolboys, appeared to have had an argument with his shoes as they hung at half-mast round his calves. His ungroomed,

## Facing up to mission impossible

greying hair was sticking up at every conceivable angle, and he sported a luxuriant growth of what is nowadays referred to as designer stubble, although in the case of this dishevelled fellow the word 'designer' was being charitable in the extreme.

As this man of mystery shuffled through the front door and headed off in the direction of the building where I was to undergo my interrogation, I concluded that he must be a client attending for therapy and I began to muse on the kind of issues he might be dealing with – lack of self-esteem and a concomitant sense of under-achievement being high on the list. Imagine my shock, or, more accurately, my state of severe traumatization, when I was eventually shown into the interview room to be confronted by the very same individual, dirty mac and carrier bag now safely tucked away out of sight, staring at me pointedly from the other side of a huge desk. It transpired that the poor downtrodden client, as I had perceived him, was not merely a tutor at the institute, but the director of the course I was applying for, to boot.

Once the course got underway, we amused ourselves imagining how this august gentleman of the therapeutic world probably spent considerable time in front of the mirror each day carefully cultivating an image of the seemingly un-cool, unworldly academic by making it appear as if he had not bothered with his appearance at all when quite obviously he had spent a good deal of time and effort doing just that.

The point of this story is not to draw attention to the sartorial characteristics of this somewhat eccentric individual per se, rather to highlight the fact that it was difficult to feel overawed by an interviewer who might normally have pinned me to my chair by tapping into unresolved superego and transference issues (i.e. evoking memories of my dominant father and a certain cruel and callous teacher), when he now appeared so utterly ordinary and fallible, and was clearly beset by very human issues of self-image like the rest of us.

When I found that this same tutor was to be my seminar leader on the course, I convinced myself that his non-threatening presence would somehow make the whole business of starting a new course of training that much easier and less anxiety-provoking. However, when I arrived on the appointed day and walked into the meeting room to take my place alongside the 15 or so other 'freshers', the butterflies were flapping around inside so frenetically it was as if they were trying to prove the validity of chaos theory in one fell swoop.

As I sat there trying to appear calm and in control of my emotions, I asked myself not for the first time why on earth I was subjecting myself to another bout of systematic mental deconstruction. There was a frisson of excitement, too, but the eagerness to take the next steps in my continuing psychic odyssey was being swamped by the kind of creeping self-doubt that will arguably resonate with almost anyone who has undertaken therapy training.

Looking round the room, I was as convinced as I could be that my fellow students would prove to be clones of Freud, Klein and Winnicott, and even more certain that their academic brilliance and therapeutic incisiveness would leave me feeling like a 5-year-old in a Mensa forum. Strange how the mind can descend to irrational depths in such circumstances. I remember on the first day of my foundation course at a different training institute, we were going through the 'getting to know you' introductions to which students are routinely subjected, when one of my fellow new boys expressed his anxiety about meeting with his new peer group. This trendily-dressed, seemingly 'together' young man amazed us all by saying: 'I was really worried about what you would all be like. I thought everyone would have better shoes than me (Freud and Man's *Sole* perhaps)'.

The concern about having the right shoes was echoed by another student on the same training course, who confessed that for some time he had been obsessed with the notion that he had to dress a certain way in order to project the 'correct' image of a therapist (perhaps he signed up for secret lessons with the aforementioned tutor), and thus ensure that he would be taken seriously, not just by his clients but by fellow students and therapists.

Responses to student questionnaires, which I distributed to a wide cross-section of past and present students in order to elicit material for this book, indicated quite clearly that there are certain key issues and concerns which are common to trainees of all levels and orientations. Underscoring the above examples of negative self-image, the issue that manifested itself most frequently with regard to beginning a therapy training was feelings of inadequacy and inferiority vis-à-vis fellows trainees.

The kinds of fantasies that can arise through an almost masochistic compulsion to compare oneself unfavourably with contemporaries are neatly summarized by Sarah Bedford, who describes her emotions on starting her training as follows:

> I assumed that everyone else would know more and would already be working in jobs where they were counselling. I thought everyone else on the course would already have dealt with all their emotional issues; that they would be open-minded, well-balanced, serene, sorted, and that I would be found wanting in those areas and would be seen as a fraud . . . The reality was quite different, needless to say.

What must also be taken into account when students compare themselves with their fellows is that there is frequently another, less passive side, more specifically the very human matter of sibling rivalry. I am not saying that all trainees regress to a point where they harbour childlike fantasies of aggression and destruction against their erstwhile 'baby sisters and brothers'. Yet whether or not we experience such negative feelings towards our contemporaries, the issue of sibling rivalry is undoubtedly a major factor. It can involve not only a feeling of having to strive for academic and clinical superiority (which possibly owes its origins to a Darwinian process of survival of the fittest, that is to say developing characteristics and strategies that will enable us to out-perform our 'siblings'), but also a subconscious need to seek 'parental' approval from tutors and supervisors, which can sometimes result in a kind of 'teacher's pet' or 'apple for the teacher' mentality.

Among the academics and trainers I interviewed to gather material for this book was Lesley Murdin, Head of Training at Westminster Pastoral Foundation, who said:

> *There is a lot of sibling rivalry in training. People start from different levels and come from many different backgrounds and they are bound to compare how much experience they have had and how quickly they grasp what is being taught. There is often a feeling that if you don't go at the pace of the fastest you're failing. They have so much to assimilate and so many changes and adaptations to make and they cannot do that to order.*

In thinking about the basis of sibling rivalry among trainees, it is useful to look at the work of Karen Horney (1937: 284–5), who offers some constructive thoughts on the nature of competitiveness and the fear of failure. In examining the link between culture and neurosis, she writes:

> *It must be emphasized . . . that competitiveness, and the potential hostility that accompanies it, pervades all human relationships . . . The potential hostile tension between individuals results in a constant generation of fear – fear of the potential hostility of others, reinforced by a fear of retaliation for hostilities of one's own. Another important source of fear in the normal individual is the prospect of failure. The fear of failure is a realistic one because, in general, the chances of failing are much greater than those of succeeding, and because failures in a competitive society entail a realistic frustration of needs. They mean not only economic insecurity, but also loss of prestige and all kinds of emotional frustrations.*

Horney helps us understand the spiralling sense of being alone and of not being good enough that can often be felt by therapy trainees when she goes on to say (1937: 286):

# On training to be a therapist

*All these factors together – competitiveness, and its potential hostilities between fellow human beings, fears, diminished self-esteem – result psychologically in the individual feeling that he is isolated . . . Emotional isolation is hard for anyone to endure; it becomes a calamity, however, if it coincides with apprehensions and uncertainties about one's self.*

This potentially destructive mixture of self-doubt and isolation is alluded to by another trainee, Mary Henderson: 'I was concerned that I would not fit into the social hierarchy of the profession, that I would not be wanted, and that I would be without friends and colleagues.' A fascinating and often neglected perspective on the issue of self-doubt and feeling an outsider is offered by a male trainee, Richard Rowell:

*My biggest fear when I began training was what it would be like to be a man in what I perceived to be a woman's world. I was aware that women are far more in touch with their emotions and I was worried that I might not be able to get in touch with mine. My ongoing concerns are: will I be good enough?*

The insidious syndrome of self-doubt also has much to do with the notion of 'getting it right', especially in the early stages of training. In other words there can be a hope or even a belief that there is a magic formula or formulae that will assuage and unlock every anxiety-provoking situation and issue, whether it be personal image, clinical practice, academic endeavour, or any one of a myriad of issues that can gnaw away at the very essence of trainees like acid eating through metal. The ever-growing preoccupation with evidence and results as a measure of therapeutic outcomes, whilst arguably a good thing from a client's point of view, only serves to foster the notion that one must strive to transmute therapy – and by implication therapy training – into an exact science with rigid guidelines and 'pat' answers for every situation.

For example, it was both amusing and worrying to hear from one of my own tutors that there has been research carried out by certain behavioural practitioners into the optimum number of head nods a therapist should make during a session. The thinking behind this almost laughable piece of therapeutic investigation – and indeed any other such narrowly-focused theory or dogma – seems to be that if you find the optimum number of times you should nod your head (or whatever else it may be) during a session you will have unmasked the eternal secret to successful therapy. If only it were that simple.

As training gets underway and we boldly venture into deep therapeutic space it is only natural that we should seek to cloak ourselves in a kind of regressive and childlike omnipotence to try to fend off the demons of doubt, or search for some sort of ultimate truth to which we can nail our therapeutic colours in the hope of appearing academically and clinically 'sorted'. However, any attempt at covering up the psychological cracks and insecurities can involve the creation of a false self, in the sense Winnicott used the term, namely adapting or inhibiting one's natural way of being to please others. In other words, we act in an incongruent or inauthentic way, based on what we feel we *should* be rather than who or what we truly are or potentially could become.

When we are in training at any level there is a reality to the notion of having to adopt at least some degree of false-self behaviour because there is a requirement to reach certain standards in order to obtain the qualification we are working towards. The assessment process to which we are subjected on these various training courses will inevitably be based at least to some extent on other people's notions of what is required academically and what it takes to be a competent therapist, so in that sense we have to play a conformist role. The difficulty and the potentially damaging effects of such compliance arises when we feel under pressure to conform to a certain way of being that feels fundamentally wrong, and to say and do certain things that may go wholly against the grain. This frequently correlates with the issues and conflicts our clients bring to therapy.

Most if not all of us have internalized a notion of an authority or superego figure, in the Freudian sense of an internalized critic. This is often a parent or teacher, from whom we learned by dictum, i.e. 'This is the way you do it. It is the only way and anything else is wrong'. That sense of needing to be fed – or even force-fed – can take a lot of expunging. And therein lies another component of student insecurity – the relative freedom and capacity for questioning that characterizes the world of therapy and its learning processes compared to, say, the academic or scientific worlds. To put it another way, it can seem strange and even disorientating not to have someone telling you what to do and what to think in every situation, as was the case in your parental home or your school or university.

Peter Lomas (1987: 123–4) talks of our propensity for viewing major figures of all kinds who control our lives as parents, and offers a caveat for trainees in regard to the parental metaphor:

> One area in which this metaphor can have damaging consequences is that of psychotherapy training, which tends to follow the traditional dichotomy between teachers who know and students who need to be given knowledge. At the Cambridge Society of Psychotherapy (often known as The Outfit) we have been trying over the

## On training to be a therapist

*past twenty years to establish a community of learning in which
the student is given the opportunity – and responsibility – for
using a facilitating environment to learn to practise therapy . . .*

*There are many forces at present in the profession and in society
that curtail the ideals of our organisation, but there is also one to
which we are all prone; the temptation to relinquish responsibility
or seek someone who will tell us what to do. There is a danger
that the parental metaphor in psychotherapy . . . may encourage
this weakness, with the consequence that students are too readily
inhibited from using their own imaginative powers.*

In this context, the whole of training could be summarized as a constant balancing act between the opinions, teachings and
demands of tutors and supervisors, and the need to maintain a core self.
In other words, allowing as little as possible of our personal qualities,
attributes, and spontaneity to be gradually eroded like the drip-drip process of water wearing away stone. It would be wrong to deny that there
are certain basic skills and attitudes that every therapist needs to espouse
and to hone; that is why we are required to undertake training. Yet,
without in any way wanting to imply arrogance or complacency, an
ability to conserve and to nurture one's own uniqueness in terms of life
experience and an understanding of people and the world is, as Lomas
has suggested, arguably more important and ultimately of more benefit
to our clients than any attempt at getting it right.

Having to think for oneself, instead of being sustained by
the constant 'drip-feed' of a more traditional academic discipline, throws
up another aspect of trainee concern, one that can run right through all
levels of training and can continue well into therapeutic 'adulthood'.
The problem in a nutshell is one of being able to stay with and sometimes to justify and defend a training and ultimately a profession which
is not only staunchly esoteric but which, in many instances, accepts
uncertainty, unknowing, and untestable and unquantifiable outcomes
as common currency.

I am sure many trainees will have experienced a sense of
awkwardness and even a feeling of being something of a fraud when
friends and family ask what exactly it is we do and what precisely we
learn during the seemingly endless years of training. I remember one of
my best friends saying to me during the latter stages of my training:
'Why on earth do you need to spend all that time training and shell out
all that money on your own therapy and supervision when all you're
really doing is sitting in a room with someone who has a problem and
trying to be a good listener? You don't really need much training for
that, do you? All you really need is a way with people.'

## Facing up to mission impossible

In the face of such uncomplicated logic, the case for the defence can seem tenuous, to say the least. It is a theme which is taken up by another of my interviewees, Dr Adrienne Baker, Academic Coordinator at Regent's College School of Psychotherapy and Counselling, as a major reason for angst amongst trainees:

> Many students have real doubts about why they're doing it. They are burdened with an increasing sense of inadequacy, but it's certainly not as clear cut as getting it right either from an academic or a therapeutic perspective. It has much more to do with making a total commitment to an indefinable process, to deal with something that feels ephemeral. It is about that connection you make with a client that feels so elusive but which feels like the essence of therapy: two souls meeting at a very profound level.
>
> So they ask themselves 'Will I ever really be able to understand why this person feels so bad about himself?' Those who come from a therapy background sometimes feel they've gone on and on asking themselves these kinds of questions and wonder if they will ever have the answers. It's almost simpler to come from a non-therapeutic background and therefore to have less need for self-questioning.

Murdin's comments, made earlier in this chapter, about trainees coming from many different backgrounds highlight another reason for the preoccupation with finding the approved or correct way of doing things. Therapy is a second career for most practitioners, and therefore most students come into training after working in another environment, often one that is totally in contrast to the world of therapy in every way. And in most, if not all, of those prior professions there is indeed an obsession with results, forecasts, prognoses, clearly definable gains and, in essence, getting it right. Whether it be medicine, commerce, advertising, legal work, or in my own case, journalism, or virtually any other field, the emphasis is very firmly on such matters as material gain, goals achieved, accuracy and client or consumer satisfaction.

When we think of the many different backgrounds of trainees and the careers they abandon in order to enter this 'curious calling', as Sussman labelled the practice of therapy in his eponymous book (1992), it is also pertinent to examine the myriad of reasons why these people decide to make the move. Besides offering a fascinating insight into the motivation of therapy practitioners and the 'pay-offs' they receive from their work, an analysis of the multiplicity of reasons for training, can I believe, shed a good deal of light on the expectations which students of psychotherapy bring to their 'apprenticeship' and how they will approach it and deal with it.

17

# On training to be a therapist

A good few square metres of rainforest have been wiped out by writers exploring the subject of therapist motivation. What follows is an overview of the most frequently cited reasons for entering the profession. The list cannot be regarded as totally comprehensive, and no doubt there will be some readers who feel their own motives have been ignored. This is to be regretted, but it is unavoidable given the complexity and diversity of the human psyche around which we have built our sometimes unfathomably curious calling.

One reason that would certainly have been conspicuous by its presence is money because it is surely verging on a truism to say that if you enter the world of therapy hoping to get rich or even to secure yourself a life of relative financial ease you are – with the exception of a very favoured few – putting yourself in line for an extremely rude awakening. Extrapolating on the view that people choose therapy as a vocation rather than a career pursued for financial or material gain, it is my personal belief that there is what might be termed a meta-psychological reason why some people enter training, especially by those who are leaving behind a previous career that is seen as increasingly pointless or unfulfilling.

This 'transcendent' syndrome concerns a universal move towards a more meaningful and enlightened way of living. Money, possessions and so many of the things espoused and lauded by the rabid greed and spiritual emptiness of the twentieth century are increasingly – if sometimes almost imperceptibly – being eschewed for the pursuit of love, truth and the common good. The relentless promotion of self and self-aggrandizement is being called more and more into question amidst a developing climate of altruism and a feeling that to give is better than to take. This is to a certain extent being manifested in the ever-increasing number of publications aimed at teaching people how to find a more meaningful lifestyle, and also the ever-swelling number of training courses for psychotherapy and counselling, healing and self-awareness.

If that sounds Pollyannaish and trite in its idealism, perhaps the cynics should not be too quick to sneer because that in itself is arguably a manifestation of the very 'disease' I have highlighted. I believe much of mankind has lost the ability to think in terms other than profit, self-advancement and instant gratification of one's own needs and desires. Attempting, through the practice of therapy, or indeed any of the helping professions, to offer help and support to others who are less able to help themselves, is arguably one small step mankind can take towards redressing the balance.

In contrast to this beneficence, it is also my belief that there is a far less magnanimous, more self-serving meta-motivation. As we race deeper into the new millennium there is a universal feeling that

# Facing up to mission impossible

events are becoming less and less subject to our control, not just in terms of world affairs but in everyday matters where bureaucracy, red tape and technological wizardry, which advances at a seemingly unstoppable pace, make individuals feel less and less significant and their lives seem more and more dehumanized and devoid of purpose.

To counter this, there are those who subconsciously perceive that one way of taking back some degree of power is to work as a therapist and thus exercise the kind of control with clients that cannot be manifested in their lives outside the consulting room. I am aware that some may vehemently reject this suggestion, but through my own experience of therapists and trainees I am convinced that some individuals, admittedly very much in the minority, are attempting to change or mould their clients, or brainwash them with their own particular dogma, in order to feel more important and more in charge of life itself. This is akin to what the eminent psychoanalyst, Ernest Jones (1951: 244) referred to as 'The God Complex'.

Leaving aside this 'bigger picture', here are the main reasons I have unearthed for training, beginning with those put forward by Francis Dale (1997: 12–15), all of which I would broadly accept. Four of Dale's categories – the challenge of the unknown/intellectual curiosity, a love of truth, interest in other people, and compassion – are fairly self-evident and do not need enlarging upon. For the rest, which follow, I have included some of Dale's explanatory material:

> *Making reparation: Many of us have, in our personal experience, been confronted with pain, misery and despair in people we are close to, or love, but have been unable to help them . . . I know, for example, of one person whose real reason for working with handicapped people stemmed from her experience of having a sister who was mentally handicapped.*
>
> *Guilt: This can arise from the same kind of situation as described in the above example. The same therapist may have been equally motivated by guilt at being the normal child or because of angry or destructive emotions directed at the sister who took up so much of her parents' time or who caused so much trouble and anxiety.*
>
> *Displacement: This refers to a psychical mechanism in which one defends oneself against having to acknowledge and suffer from one's own hidden pathology by displacing, projecting, or locating it in someone else.*
>
> *Omnipotent control: This is frequently related to displacement and is based on a fear or even terror of whatever one is avoiding inside of oneself.*

**19**

## On training to be a therapist

**Sadism:** *This frequently occurs in tandem with omnipotent control and displacement. Not only are parts of the self that are experienced as threatening to one's stability split off and projected into someone else, but they are also cruelly manipulated, controlled, attacked and frequently denigrated.*

**Vicarious healing:** *In this situation, the therapist vicariously heals himself through the healing part of the patient he is in unconscious identification with. [Author's note: this correlates with the universal concept of the 'wounded healer', who is able to empathize because of his own traumatic or negative experiences, and, in the process, may subconsciously secure healing for him or herself].*

**Vicarious living:** *Here, the therapist . . . experiences life, at its greatest intensity, 'through his relationship with his patients'. That is, he lives his life using his patients' life experiences rather than his own.*

Alice Miller (1987: 45–6) takes a thought-provoking line when she writes about certain common factors in therapists' histories and, in so doing, issues a warning (which will be elaborated on in the next chapter) that should be heeded by trainees of all levels:

> *It is often said that psychotherapists suffer from an emotional disturbance . . . The therapist's sensibility, empathy, responsiveness, and powerful 'antennae' indicate that as a child he probably used to fulfill others people's needs and to repress his own . . .*
>
> *I think that our childhood fate can indeed enable us to practice psychotherapy, but only if we have been given the chance, through our own therapy, to live with the reality of our past and to give up the most flagrant of our illusions. This means tolerating the knowledge that, to avoid losing the 'love' of our parents, we were compelled to gratify their unconscious needs at the cost of our own emotional development.*
>
> *It also means being able to experience the resentment and mourning aroused by our parents' failure to fufil our primary needs. If we have never consciously lived through this despair and the resulting rage, and have therefore never been able to work through it, we will be in danger of transferring this situation, which would then remain unconscious, onto our patients.*

Pursuing this theme, Miller goes on later (1987: 49):

## Facing up to mission impossible

*Only after painfully experiencing and accepting our own truth can we be free from the hope that we might still find an understanding, empathic 'parent' – perhaps in a patient – who will be at our disposal. The temptation to seek a parent among our patients should not be underestimated; our own parents seldom or never listened to us with such rapt attention as our patients usually do, and they never revealed their inner world to us as clearly and honestly as do our patients at times.*

If Miller highlights the temptation to misuse and even abuse our clients as part of our unconscious motivation, Herbert Strean (1991: 10–11) goes much further:

*Because the analyst's fantasies and fears in the analytic situation have remained so secret, few people really know what makes an analyst tick . . . Though analysts would be the first to speak of the voyeurism of an obstetrician or gynaecologist, who looks at naked bodies all day, they do not discuss the voyeuristic pleasure they derive as they peer at people who are emotionally naked on the couch . . .*

*Altruism is easy to talk about. Most people who help others say they are interested in enhancing the lives of those they help. But this is an incomplete explanation of their motives. If analysts are really truthful they would also have to acknowledge a certain superiority that surfaces and says in essence to a patient, 'I'm glad I'm not you. I feel stronger and more competent in facing life.' There is also the opposite feeling: many times I have said to myself as a listened to a patient, 'There but for the grace of God lie I'. Or from time to time I have envied patients who appeared sharper and more insightful than I.*

Miller's references to personal therapy point to another reason for people training – that of wanting to become a therapist because of insights and therapeutic gain achieved in their own therapy. One danger of this particular motivation is over-identification with and idealization of their therapist and idealization of the therapeutic process. Carl Goldberg (1993: 85) addresses the potential problems for this type of practitioner, who is overly grateful for what they regard as 'life saving' interventions of their therapist:

*Some of these fervently dedicated practitioners have never resolved in their personal psychotherapy a pervasive denial of their feelings of unworthiness. They see themselves through the eyes of their therapist. In this light they are appalled by their desperation, dependency, and deep oral craving. To deny this painful picture of themselves they have become 'as if' people. They desperately try to convince themselves they 'are' their therapist . . . To maintain this 'as if salvation', they find practical ways to become psychotherapists themselves.*

To round off this review of therapist motivation, it seems appropriate to quote from a book by Lesley Murdin (2000: 78) about endings in therapy. Talking of clients who end unilaterally, she writes:

*Most therapists when left in this way feel injured, abandoned, mystified, undervalued . . . Therapists have to be able to deal with the feelings aroused in themselves and to try to learn what they can from the experience . . . One of the reasons for undertaking this profession is, I suspect, that therapists desire to learn to cope with loss, since it is our constant professional experience.*

Having looked at a wide range of objective thought on therapist motivation, it would seem incomplete to close this section without some subjective input from trainees. The following responses to my student questionnaires offer what I hope is a fairly comprehensive cross-section of reasons for training.

*Ewan Gillon: Before I trained I suppose I saw counselling as a way of enabling me to contribute toward the well-being of others in a way that suited my background and personality. However, the transition to becoming a counsellor was a lot more complex than I had realized and the training linked into all sorts of issues regarding who I am and how I relate to others. Looking back I can see my desire to be a counsellor as partly an escape mechanism because it offers an intimacy that may be missing in everyday life, and partly as a channel for an element of myself that I actually value.*

*Natalie Gibb: I wanted to train as a therapist as it offers me an opportunity to experience myself as an authentic human being and to offer a space in which clients may experience some of what it is like to access an internal place whereby one does not have to construct oneself into what is required, that it is simply enough 'to be'. Being involved in counsellor training also affords me continual spiritual, intellectual and emotional growth.*

*Riann Croft: I work best at 'micro-level'. I have strong world views, primarily about justice, fairness and choice, but I find it*

## Facing up to mission impossible

*overwhelming and depressing to try to change the world at macro (economic/political) level, so I work with people on a personal level.*

***Mary Henderson:*** *To be able to be in employment which is challenging and satisfying. Working as a psychotherapist is not work, but it is a vocation and it gives my life meaning and value.*

As I have already indicated above, there are almost certainly other reasons why people become therapists. However, the object of the exercise was not to nail down every possible constituent of therapist motivation, but rather to highlight the myriad of often unconscious factors leading to the decision to train in the first place. It seemed important to focus on this area at the beginning of the book because by examining our motives, bringing the unconscious ones to consciousness and working through them, it can make us better therapists in terms of our ability to work exclusively for the good of the client, rather than seeking to benefit from the encounter by proxy. Yet that is by no means the full rationale for this process of self-examination, about which more will be said in the next chapter when discussing personal therapy.

Questioning our motivation can help us to think more deeply about why we really find ourselves sitting anxiously in a room full of other trainees, embarking on this long and difficult road. And, as training clicks into gear, to re-examine on an ongoing basis and with complete honesty the key question about why we originally entered training. This can help us to identify the true goal of our training, whatever that individual target might be, and can enable us to pursue that process in a more satisfying and productive way.

First and foremost it is necessary to ask ourselves whether we really do want to work as a therapist. Dealing with unhappy and often seriously disturbed people day in and day out can be as debilitating as it is rewarding. There is also the associated question of whether we are prepared to pay a potentially huge price in personal terms (this will also be expanded on in Chapter 2). If the answer is 'no' or we are not totally convinced, then we might need to consider whether we are doing the training purely for personal growth, or are taking the course to learn about a subject that fascinates us but does not appeal as a vocation. Then again, perhaps we simply enjoy undertaking this type of training course as an interactive process which offers the prospect of meeting like-minded people and bonding with them in a way that is often impossible in our everyday world.

All of these motives for training are equally valid in their way. But whatever the reason I would urge you to know yourself in this respect. Self-deception will lead to frustration, disappointment and bitterness. I have seen more than one person on my own training courses exhibiting those emotions to a point where they were not only harming themselves but also upsetting and hindering their fellow students. As trainee therapists we should be able to work with such disturbances, it is true, but my point is that the angst was almost certainly due to the fact that these people based their expectations on false notions of what they were seeking, so the anger and recriminations were, to a certain extent, avoidable.

Trainees can, of course, suffer bad experiences simply by dint of circumstance. For example being landed with a narcissistic or sadistic tutor or facilitator, or an unempathic supervisor. The way in which students are inducted and welcomed onto the course can also have a huge bearing on their perceptions and their ongoing emotional state. Take, for example, this summary by Anne Green of her early experiences of a psychodynamic training.

> On the first day we were divided into two sets for the personal development group and marched into two different rooms. It was like the Gestapo. I was terrified because I didn't have a clue about what was going to happen. The tutors were all totally blank screen, so I played the clown as a kind of defence. Then it transpired that a guy in my group was an alcoholic and he fell in love with a girl in the group. He was thrown off the course for coming in drunk and she then left. We ended up hacking our way through the personal development group and I eventually left after the first year because of a tutor who was very unempathic and narcissistic.

In working towards the end of this opening chapter, it is necessary to admit that up to this point the material has largely been based on negative assumptions, principally the premise that undertaking therapy training causes, amongst other things, anxiety, self-doubt and even humiliation. It would therefore only be proper to offer the whole picture – after all this book was designed, as I have said in the introduction, to enable trainees to get the most out of training, and even to enjoy it! There are those who sail through their training seemingly without turning a therapeutic hair and who are totally convinced from the beginning that they are on the right path. So here are three examples of positive student feedback to help set the record straight.

> **Jane Gilmore:** I was excited about the prospect of training. I usually find training courses stimulating. I am usually motivated to undertake a course by my perceived need, e.g. before I started

## Facing up to mission impossible

*my diploma I was working as a breast cancer counsellor (I came from a nursing background) and I felt that I had inadequate skills and knowledge to further my work in this field. I therefore identified a course that would fulfil those needs. I also had unconscious motivations, some of which could have been to gain a deeper understanding of myself, to meet like-minded people, and to give myself an intellectual challenge.*

**Alan Sanders:** *I was lucky in being part of a very supportive group of students who trained together. Our course leader stressed the importance of treating each other with care on such courses in his introductory talk to our group. People have told me this allayed their fears, as it did mine.*

**Jan Waterman:** *I had no particular fears or concerns when I began training. My only emotions were the pleasurable anticipation of learning and meeting new people.*

I genuinely salute these and others like them, but it is my firm belief, backed up by my research amongst a wide cross-section of trainees, that whether you scythe through your training and come bouncing back for more, or find it burdensome and angst-ridden from the start, or fall somewhere between the two, there will be periods for all trainees when doubt and anxiety is felt in varying degrees. That is unless you are the very model of a therapeutic automaton, who is impervious to the huge emotional and logistical demands that are an integral part of training courses – and a therapeutic robot is, of course, the antithesis of what a good therapist should be.

In this context, I recall being much gratified by the response of my supervisor at a psychiatric placement which I had just started. After listening to me expressing a high degree of anxiety about working with this new group of patients, many of whom were seriously disturbed, my supervisor replied, 'That's good to hear. I would be worried if you weren't anxious', adding with a heartening degree of empathy, 'Do you think the anxiety ever goes away?'

It was refreshing indeed to hear my supervisor's admission of the ongoing struggle, something echoed by Nina Coltart (1992: 2) when she wrote, 'It is of the essence of our impossible profession that in a very singular way we do not know what we are doing'. I believe Coltart was exaggerating in order to make a point, namely that we so often have to stay with uncertainty and feelings of therapeutic impotence. Obviously we need to have some idea or fundamental concept of what we are attempting to achieve or we could not be in any way effective.

## On training to be a therapist

However, when we begin our journey, and progress along the road, we should endeavour not to be too hard on ourselves. Feeling inadequate, small, unworthy, lost and alone, or a combination of all of these, is not merely normal but could also be said to indicate an attitude that is desirable and healthy in terms of the capacity for self-questioning and self-reflection, which a good therapist needs. It is also perfectly okay to experience feelings of being deconstructed, undermined, or got at, and being perceived as different, or even slightly weird – all of which leads us neatly into Chapter 2 . . .

# 2     A change for the better?

The scenario I am about to describe will, I am sure, be familiar to many people who have undergone psychotherapy or counselling training. The verbal exchanges and the reactions may differ in matters of detail and content, but the nature of the interaction and the sentiments behind it epitomize, I believe, the interface between those who practice, or are learning to practice, psychotherapy and the rest of the world who do not.

The situation in question arose at a particularly tedious dinner party into which I allowed myself to be inveigled against my better judgement not long before I began writing this book. I have found myself in similar situations and encounters before and after this particular one, but the essence of this little interlude of verbal ping-pong across a crowded dinner table sums up perfectly for me the kinds of immutable perceptions and assumptions held by what may be loosely termed 'non-therapeutic' persons regarding the custom and practice, the rationale and the character of our curious profession.

As the coffee and the mints were being handed round and the seemingly ceaseless round of mindless small talk descended to new levels of banality, I suddenly and unwittingly obtained instant relief from my escalating boredom when, in response to the fairly standard 'What do you do for a living?' question, I happened to reveal my 'other life' as a trainee therapist. I say 'happened' because I have grown wary over the years of letting this piece of information slip for reasons that will become all too apparent in the succeeding paragraphs.

# On training to be a therapist

No sooner had the word 'psychotherapist' left my lips than there were wide-eyed looks, sharp intakes of breath and knowing smiles. These in turn were followed by an extraordinary sequence of reactions ranging from the cynical to the aggressive to the nudge, nudge, wink, wink variety.

'Oh, so you're one of those, 'said one guest, who had seemed quite rational and tolerant up to that point. 'I suppose you can read my mind. So, go on, tell me – what am I thinking at this moment?'

'Contrary to popular belief, psychotherapists are not magicians,' I said. 'We don't read people's minds. What we are doing in simple terms is trying to help people get their minds back on track.'

'I'll bet you are,' another guest chimed in with a sneer. 'A dirt track, no doubt. I've heard about you psychoanalysts or whatever you like to call yourselves. It's all that Freudian stuff – sex, sex, and more sex.'

I was about to inform this irritating individual that Freud's apparent obsession with sexual motivation had been widely distorted and taken out of context over the years when a third member of our little soirée – again a seemingly logical and affable individual up to that point – jumped in feet first.

'I don't believe in all that psychology rubbish,' he said. 'Most of it's a complete con – and a very lucrative one at £50 an hour or whatever the going rate is. Get a grip and get on with it, I say. The problem is we're all far too obsessed with navel-gazing and self-analysis these days. In my opinion there's nothing going on up here (he pointed to his head) that a good stiff drink won't cure.' He took a large swig of his brandy and settled back in his chair with a self-satisfied smirk on his face.

At this point I gave up and decided a policy of polite humouring was the most sensible course of action, even though it felt as if I had run up the white flag without any serious attempt at defending myself and my profession. Isn't it ironic, I thought, here we are in an age of so-called enlightenment and yet many people are still so afraid of anything remotely concerned with the functioning of the mind (or should that be malfunctioning?) that they lose all reason and judgement at the merest mention of the subject. Depression, broken relationships and suicides are spiralling and yet offering or seeking any kind of professional help in that direction is still regarded by many folk as stigmatizing, namby-pamby rubbish, or even manipulative and harmful.

Despite my attempts to dismiss this thoroughly forgettable evening from my thoughts, the reactions of my fellow guests had left their mark in one major way. As I tried unsuccessfully to laugh off the banter and the brickbats, I recalled a comment from a friend, who had undertaken a therapy training herself. On hearing of my decision to

## A change for the better?

begin my own training, she stated portentously, 'It will change your life, John'.

What on earth could she mean, I wondered, little realizing that the answer would reveal itself far sooner than I could possibly have expected. I was to discover that my friend had been talking not merely about change in terms of other people's perceptions of us and our own perceptions of ourselves, but also about our whole way of being in the world and interacting with others. The external ramifications of becoming 'one of them', as exemplified by the outpourings at the dinner table, are one thing; the sea changes inside, which are engendered by training, quite another.

The process once begun can never be halted. It is like a truck with no brakes picking up speed down a long and winding hill. You can steer to a certain extent, but trying to keep to the road is another matter. Indeed there are many times when it feels like you will drop off it altogether. Another client failing to show, or what feels like a particularly devastating comment from a supervisor, are two of the more obvious destabilizers, but how we see ourselves vis-à-vis the world and the way in which our relationships are altered, put under pressure or even systematically dismantled, can be far more insidious and undermining.

Self-questioning and ensuing self-deprecation can lead to a downward spiral as we feel ourselves becoming more and more estranged from the rest of the human race. Relationships can be increasingly put under strain as partners feel threatened, long-standing friendships can suddenly seem shallow, indeed the whole world outside the cosy little microcosm of therapy can appear increasingly fatuous.

Or is it us? That is the most teasing question of all. When partners, friends and children start coming out with remarks like 'For God's sake stop analysing me', or 'Your problem is that you've lost touch with the real world', it is difficult not to wonder if they are the more perceptive ones.

This self-questioning can lead to all kinds of worrying fantasies about the creatures we will eventually become – if we have not done so already. Will we be so immersed in the seductive imbroglio of endless analysis and mind games that we totally lose sight of Freud's putative dictum 'Sometimes a cigar is just a cigar' (this cannot be found in any of Freud's writings and is therefore taken to be apocryphal)? Will we sit at the breakfast table delivering little gems to our partners like 'I'm wondering why you accused me of giving you a small helping of cereal this morning. Perhaps your father was a bit mean with the Weetabix.'?

Another strange phenomenon of therapy training is that people suddenly imagine we should have all the answers, not just to the problems of others but to our own difficulties as well. 'How can someone who calls himself a therapist have marital difficulties or teenagers from hell?', we hear them ask. 'Surely with their therapeutic antennae they should be able to nip those kinds of problems in the bud'. The curious thing is that although we know omniscience is impossible we often feel guilty that we do not have all the right answers; and this sense of failure is felt even more acutely in our work with our clients.

It could be said that training as a therapist necessitates a form of personal deconstruction followed by a process which involves building an entirely new way of thinking and being. It is not only this need for incessant analysis of our own reactions and those of others – whether it be in clinical work, supervision or interactions with peers – that is responsible for the systematic dismantling of self. Personal therapy, a requirement of most training courses, can, in the early stages at least, chip away at the very basis of our self-construct. Furthermore, our interactions with clients, especially the more deeply troubled ones, can be psychically debilitating and disturbing however much we may have worked on our own issues in therapy and however much we are supported in supervision.

The critical aspect of this process is that during the deconstruction phase we should take care not to throw the therapeutic baby out with the bath water. In other words, whilst allowing the new attitudes and ways of being in the world and being with others to flow in, we must avoid letting go of the more positive and psychically desirable or valuable aspects of our lives and our core selves, both in personal and clinical terms. That is something that is all too easy to allow by default when we feel racked with self-doubt, worse than useless in our encounters with clients, and under pressure from and disenchanted with relationships.

Much has been written in a negative way about the phenomenon of personal changes during training, but it is my contention that not nearly enough emphasis has been placed on the positive aspects of these changes. I have to admit that before I began work on this book my own perceptions of the way in which training affects relationships in particular had been somewhat blinkered, leaning heavily towards a presumption that therapy training inevitably means a deterioration in the quality of interaction with others and marriage/sexual partnerships in particular. This has been underpinned by the findings of certain writers and practitioners who have made it their business to carry out much-needed research into this field (as documented later in this chapter), but it is a false picture, as I will make clear.

In looking first at the potential downside of changes engendered by training, here are some replies which were either wholly or

# A change for the better?

largely negative in response to the questions 'How do you feel training has changed you as a person?' and 'How has training affected your relationships?', as contained in my student questionnaires:

> **Rita Jones:** *I've gained in confidence, self-esteem, assertiveness, physical and mental health, knowledge, skills, experience and stamina, and above all in understanding people. At times the change process has been extremely difficult for me, and the experience of my peers has been similar. I continue to be, at times, disappointed that my much improved awareness has left me acutely aware of the painful parts of my experience, rather than warm, fuzzy self-actualization as Rogers et al. seemed to promise all those years ago. Existential angst instead of the 'good life' . . . My own personal therapy has been essential to my survival.*

> **Naomi Phillips:** *It probably helped to break up my first marriage by continuing a process that was already happening. In training you open up to others and if you start to demand that of people who aren't used to that way of relating it can be a huge strain for them. The constant demand for communication from someone who isn't into communication is tough. It can also be a big strain on family, friends and children, mainly because of the demands on time and money. There are huge sacrifices to be made.*

> **Brett Maple:** *Training made me more dissatisfied with my life. I gained some understanding of reasons for human behaviour, but I lost out in terms of time and money, and it made my relationships more difficult and distant.*

In considering the negative aspects of change on therapy trainees from a more objective standpoint, let us turn first to the work of Graham Dexter, who thoroughly researched this whole area for his PhD thesis entitled 'A critical review of the effects of counselling training on trainees'. In an article for *Counselling News* (1999: 3), Dexter gave a brief overview of his perception of the dangers of training, focusing particularly on the pressure to achieve greater self-awareness as part of training courses:

> *Counselling training and its experiential nature is built on the belief that it is useful to study one's own self in order to understand ways of helping others develop their selves. But there may also be some inherent risks in self-awareness. For example, in the wake of increased self-awareness and a greater knowledge and understanding of the values important to oneself, may come an*

## On training to be a therapist

*accompanying self-condemnation produced by recrimination of past behaviour. With a more intimate understanding of what is important and meaningful in one's life may come disillusionment with present relationships, behaviours and daily life. The mundane and ordinary existence of the individual may seem less than satisfactory and this, in turn, may prompt behaviour that may lead to disengagement from some social settings. My research has suggested that on long-term courses, students construed people close to them more negatively than before. This can have serious implications for the personal life of the trainee.*

In another article from the same publication (1998: 7), David Williams and Judi Irving, of the counsellor training unit at Hull University, go even further:

*The generally accepted dictum, and one that we hold to be true, is that personal development work is risky. For 'By definition . . . self exploration leads to new discoveries and often sudden movements into unknown psychological territories. Some of these developments are likely to be disturbing and disorientating . . .' (Dryden & Thorne, 1991, p16). We would go further and say that it is not only risky, but very risky. So much so that counsellor training should probably carry a government health warning. Our personal experience testifies to the damage that can be done, and there is also growing empirical evidence of the dangers. For example, Macaskill and Macaskill (1992) showed in a UK survey that 30 per cent of trainee psychotherapists experienced negative effects of personal therapy, including personal, marital and family distress.*

Despite these dire warnings from people who have vast experience in the field, it would, as I said earlier in this chapter, paint a totally false picture to talk only of a deleterious process, with trainees staggering under a burden of strained and broken relationships, burgeoning self-doubt and confusion. Responses to my questionnaires indicated many positive aspects of change as well as negative ones. Here is a brief selection:

***Alan Sanders:*** *All gain. I used to feel inadequate if I didn't have solutions to friends' problems. No longer. I feel better equipped for life! I understand myself and have a better understanding and tolerance of others. On the first day of my counselling course we were warned that the training would have an effect on key relationships. All courses should issue such warnings. Many students were struggling in this area when I met my partner on the course.*

## A change for the better?

*Our relationship has benefited enormously from our training, but they felt they were developing and leaving their partners behind.*

**Joe Stanley:** *I have gained more understanding of my needs and more willingness to be open with less than 'lovely' feelings. I have lost some sort of level of patience/tolerance for polite behaviour! Training strengthened my most intimate relationships and made me question some others. It made me feel less willing to put myself last.*

**Sandra Walton:** *I am happier, calmer and generally enjoy my life much more – I am more fulfilled. I have lost the feeling of being a victim, I am more outspoken about my needs. I have become disappointed with some long-term friendships and have moved on and made new friends who are more on my wavelength. My marriage has improved.*

**Jane Cramp:** *I feel more congruent and authentic. I am more aware of my needs and more accepting of myself and others. I am less stressed and I am happy now to be 'good enough'.*

It is my belief that with hindsight even some of those who indicated negative consequences of training on their lives might concede that to a degree the turmoil and the angst was merely highlighted or exacerbated by training, not a direct consequence of it (I say more about this later). Indeed, in some cases, they might even agree that what seemed painful and deconstructive at the time was necessary and ultimately led them along a better path.

In looking at the overall ramifications of personal change, the point to stress above all is that when a person undertakes psychotherapy or counselling training there *will* be changes, some for the better, some for worse, and frequently a combination of the two. It is essential therefore that trainees should be aware that to a greater or lesser degree they are embarking on an emotional roller-coaster when they begin training. The process builds on itself, so it can be argued that whilst the effects of this roller-coaster ride may gradually lessen, the feeling of being bounced around psychically may take a long time to subside, and for some people the upheaval may never fully end.

Dexter takes up this point when he writes (1999: 3):

*It is equally possible that self-awareness brings great benefits for determining change for the better in all regards. The point, in essence, is that the outcome of self-awareness is uncertain and cannot be predetermined, thus it cannot be assumed that it will be 'a good thing'. What is certain, however, is that change will occur and will often be of a significant degree.*

# On training to be a therapist

As any therapist worth his salt will tell you, any change in a client, even if it is ostensibly for the better, can be destabilizing in itself. For example, in my work with problem gamblers I have frequently found that when a client gives up gambling he is fazed, often overwhelmingly, by the strangely stable nature of his world and the unfamiliar feeling of a lack of turmoil and angst with which he or she is now faced. The sense of disorientation and 'thrownness' can be especially strong when the client's self-esteem is low and the addictive/self-destructive behaviour has been used to reinforce a negative self-image and/or a feeling that everything in his or her world is destined to fail. In some such cases, a move towards a more settled and ultimately fulfilling way of life can simply be too much to handle.

David Smail (2001: 200, original emphasis) offers another perspective on change:

> There is an added complication to a belated trust in one's own experience, to acknowledging, say, that one is not the passive victim of an illness ('anxiety state') but rather the vulnerable contributor to a network of complicated and dangerous relationships. For in making any such acknowledgement, which entails beginning to take responsibility for those aspects of one's own conduct which contribute to one's predicament, it becomes immediately apparent that time formerly spent in self-deception was **wasted** time. Admitting that one was wrong, even over trivial matters, is never a particularly comfortable experience; admitting that one has made life-long mistakes and entertained entirely misleading assumptions about matters of vital personal importance is all the more painful, and constitutes often a major stumbling block to the development of a more accurate perception of the meaning of one's conduct.

In the context of relationships, it can be said that psychic change in one partner, whatever the nature and degree of that change, is bound in some degree to affect the relationship itself because the partnership is based on certain ways of relating that have been tacitly agreed, negotiated, or perhaps imposed unilaterally, and acted on over time. Thus, if a partner who has been lacking in self-esteem suddenly becomes more self-confident and outgoing it may well lead to the other partner feeling threatened, unless that individual has exorcised their own demons in that respect and feels very secure in themselves.

In this context, it can be helpful to look at some of the basic concepts of family therapy. The idea that change in an individual member of a family can fundamentally affect the dynamics of the family system as a whole is alluded to by Brown and Pedder (1994: 147–8):

## A change for the better?

*Changes in a family system may lead to distress in members other than the presenting patient, as they come to face their own responsibility for the problems and their own personal difficulties. The reality that they have sought to avoid, say the poverty of their marriage, or the loss of their children's dependence on them, may be hard to face, and require a good deal of adjustment . . . One of the possible outcomes of a family or marital approach that has to be faced, may be a decision to split up.*

This last point brings me back to my earlier suggestion that when relationships are felt to be under increasing strain during training it is often not the course itself that has brought about the stress or the rift. In many cases training merely serves to highlight a difficulty or an issue that was already there when the individual began therapy training. In these cases training is simply a catalyst for change. For the trainee to blame the course for the angst he or she is now suffering is often a projection subconsciously designed to locate the blame for the break-up outside the relationship itself. This kind of projecting can also involve the training partner saying something like 'My partner doesn't like me training' when he or she is really the one feeling anxious or destabilized.

One of the reasons why partners often feel threatened, has, I believe, much to do with the esoteric nature of therapy and therapy training courses. If the non-participating partner knows nothing about the world of therapy, he or she can find the language, the practice, indeed the whole amorphous gamut of training totally outside their normal frame of reference. Training can sometimes appear akin to a secret society where partners disappear for whole days or evenings to carry out curious, non-definable activities with sympathetic peers in an atmosphere of intimacy and openness rarely encountered at home.

Money can also be a huge factor in relationships with partners, especially when, as is often the case, only one partner is working and the working partner is paying for the other to take the course. This type of arrangement can all too obviously lead to feelings of resentment and guilt, respectively.

Training can also have an affect on our children, especially in adolescence. Teenagers are notoriously secretive and the thought of a parent suddenly developing an ability to 'see inside their head' can be quite scary for them. I well remember the reactions of my youngest son, who was in his early teens when I began my training. He was very obviously unsettled by my delving deeply into psychic matters, and I believe his angst and his search for a sense of self, which afflicts all teenagers, was certainly not helped by his perceptions of me as a kind of 'thought policeman'. On a lighter note, I also remember him saying to

## On training to be a therapist

me, 'Dad, when you become a psychotherapist, or whatever it is you're going to become, will you talk all posh and wear a monocle?' Clearly he had introjected a mental picture of a certain Sigmund Freud!

Friendships can be put under strain during training for the same reason as relationships with partners. The fact that trainees are so busy with academic assignments, clinical work and the sundry demands of courses means that they are simply not able to devote as much time or energy to friendships as they did before. The question of money arises here, too, in as much as many students are struggling to make ends meet and therefore do not have the financial resources available to maintain their previous level of social activities.

It is perhaps a less palatable truth that the self-examination and the changes engendered by training can cause trainees to look at friendships in a new and more unfavourable light. I am well aware that there is a danger of sounding self-satisfied and elitist, or even of espousing a kind of blinkered idealism. However, there is clear evidence, as alluded to by Dexter, and also born out of my own experiences and those of other students, that many trainees often find existing relationships – even those sustained over a considerable period of time – increasingly unfulfilling and shallow. This sense of dissatisfaction can be gradual and almost imperceptible for a time as we swap what increasingly feels like a relatively superficial type of relating, characterized by small talk and social niceties, for what we perceive to be a more meaningful, honest and open way of being with others.

I am not saying there is anything wrong with small talk or social interaction in itself, far from it, but it is my belief that those who opt to train as therapists are consciously or unconsciously seeking something more than the 'surface' life they have been used to up to that point. When they discover they are on the path to a deeper, more meaningful way of relating to themselves, others and the world, it is virtually impossible to step back into the old way of being. And why, one has to ask, would they want to? Nirvana it might not be, but this more real and knowing way of getting through life has the addictive quality of feeling right, even if it is beset to a certain extent with anxiety and uncertainty. It is akin to what Joseph Campbell referred to in his memorable book *The Power of Myth* (1988: 91) as 'following your bliss'. Campbell puts it this way:

> *If you follow your bliss, you put yourself on a kind of track that has been there all the while, waiting for you, and the life that you ought to be living is the one you are living. Wherever you are – if you are following your bliss, you are enjoying that refreshment, that life within you, all the time.*

## A change for the better?

This 'new way' can lead to a kind of hiatus at the end of training in which the trainee, or graduate as he or she now is, can feel caught in a kind of limbo. The 'old' life has not been totally discarded and the cloak of newness does not yet sit happily on his or her shoulders. It is necessary to state that there is a possible danger here, as encapsulated in Melanie Klein's concept of splitting, that is to say idealizing and denigrating as a defence mechanism that militates against a process of integration (Hinshelwood 1991). To reject one's previous way of being whilst building up the 'therapeutically sorted' new way is fraught with danger, principally that of denial and disillusionment. To integrate both ways would, in most cases, be the ideal result of training and, of course, many trainees manage this very successfully.

As a very real antidote to the preceding negativity, it is equally clear that change can be beneficial to relationships. When a partner is forced to look at him or herself and their part in the relationship, as a result of changes in the other, it does not always mean denial and/or conflict. Initially, there may well be fear over the perceived differences in the personality and character of the trainee and what that might mean for the relationship. However, if the non-participating partner has a sufficiently strong sense of self and is motivated to respond to the challenge of change, it may well be possible to reframe the relationship into a healthier one based on more 'real' and ultimately more respectful ways of being together.

From the point of view of trainees, a burgeoning capacity for greater insight into unconscious processes and ways of relating can obviously be of great benefit, both to the trainees themselves and their relationships. If we can understand why we behave as we do, and why partners, friends and children behave as they do, it can foster a greater sense of tolerance and love. I have found this to be particularly true of children, especially teenagers going through their stroppy 'I hate the world and especially my boring, unreasonable parents' stage. If we understand that teenagers are going through horrendous identity crises and desperately needing to develop a feeling of belonging, and that their 'impossible' behaviour is part of their struggle to separate from their parents, it can certainly make the war of attrition to which parents often feel subjected, seem less of a personal attack.

Insight gained through training and personal therapy can also shed light on day-to-day interactions in a way that can be both revealing and helpful. For example, I recall how a friend of mine would often ring me up and, in response, to my 'Hello' he would say, 'You sound really depressed' or a variation on that theme. For a long time, I would take this on board and would end up berating myself and questioning whether I came across generally as a depressed and boring person.

# On training to be a therapist

As I came to understand the concept of projection through my clinical work and my training, I realized he was projecting his own depressed feelings into me. I was able to respond to his accusation by saying, 'No, actually I'm fine. Maybe you're the one that's really feeling depressed.' After a poignant silence, he replied: 'Perhaps you're right. I do feel quite down.'

From a professional perspective, it can be said that for a therapist to remain in a state of psychic stasis – that is, not attempting through self-exploration to refine and enlarge his understanding of himself, his relationships and the world around him – would not only be a barrier to good practice but would be grossly irresponsible as well.

A therapist who does not at least attempt to deal with their own pathology, especially their psychic blocks, will have trouble offering their clients the most basic preconditions for good therapy, such as empathy and unconditional positive regard, when the client brings material that taps into the therapist's own unresolved issues. They will certainly be less available to their clients emotionally because they are preoccupied with or blinded by their own demons.

This is where we come to the notion of countertransference, and whilst there is neither the room nor the need to delve too deeply into this phenomenon for the purposes of this book, it is worth looking at some of its basic precepts as they apply to the issue of self-exploration. The notion of countertransference was introduced by Freud, who saw it as an impediment to the analytic process. However, that idea has been almost totally reversed in recent times and it is now widely regarded as one of the most helpful psychotherapeutic phenomena, if used correctly.

Charles Rycroft, in his *Critical Dictionary of Psychoanalysis* (1995: 28–9), defines countertransference as:

> *1. The analyst's transference on his patient. In this, the correct, sense, countertransference is a disturbing, distorting element in treatment. 2. By extension, the analyst's emotional attitude towards his patient, including his response to specific items of the patient's behaviour. According to Heimann (1950), Little (1951), Gitelson (1952), and others, the analyst can use this latter kind of countertransference as clinical evidence, i.e. he can assume that his own emotional response is based on a correct interpretation of the patient's true intentions or meaning . . .*

Herbert Strean (1991: 6–7) embellishes this definition in a very human way (as in virtually all such examples, the words 'psychotherapist' or 'counsellor' can easily be substituted for the term 'analyst' throughout):

## A change for the better?

*For many years I have felt that unless I could permit myself to free associate to my patient's expressed thoughts and words and constantly explore what I was feeling in the analytic process, I could not really be of much help to the patient . . . As the analyst experiences this wide range of human emotions, he reacts with a wide range of emotions. Yet no analyst has yet written of what he subjectively feels or thinks when a patient praises or attacks him . . . One of my main purposes in writing this book is to show that the psychoanalyst is fundamentally a human being . . . Let's face it: psychoanalysts eat, sleep, go to the bathroom, experience feelings of love and hate, elation and depression . . .*

The point that all therapists are human (some clients might dispute this!) means that even if the therapist has undergone extensive personal therapy, it is not always easy to bracket instinctive reactions to patients. However, it is necessary to make a distinction between two different types of countertransference feelings, as highlighted by Petrūska Clarkson (1999: 89):

*Countertransference is nowadays divided between what the psychotherapist brings – what can be termed proactive countertransference (really pathological psychotherapist transference on to the client) – and that to which the psychotherapist reacts in the patient often termed reactive or inductive countertransference.*

She elucidates by saying (1999: 92):

*It is essential that the clinician be able to separate out proactive from reactive countertransference within this paradigm. Then it becomes possible and effective to use reactive countertransference as information about the expected or anticipated patterns of the patient, rather than confuse it with organismic data about the psychotherapist's own life or feelings or their own historical needs and expectations.*

*One hopes that psychotherapists will have resolved most of the major ways in which their own pathology or unresolved archaic experiences might interfere with their work with patients. However, since few of us fully resolve all of our personal issues completely and permanently, it is important that we at least understand ourselves enough to be able to identify and counteract our own pathological patterns, especially countertransferential responses based on unresolved issues from our own past.*

# On training to be a therapist

Joyce McDougall (1986: 285) echoes this last issue when she writes:

*Are shortcomings in analytic treatment due to unconscious dissimulations, weaknesses in our theory, or the vicissitudes of countertransference interference? The last element certainly constitutes one of our greatest stumbling blocks: every analyst is keenly aware of the risk of listening too closely to his or her own inner beliefs and expectations, knowing that these may deflect the analytic discourse and transmit to the patient problems that belong to the analyst.*

So, based on the almost universally held view that unresolved therapist issues can not only hinder treatment but also damage the client, it must surely be right for trainees to undergo some form of protracted self-exploration. Not everyone will agree that this is necessarily best achieved through personal therapy, however. As indicated earlier there is evidence that personal therapy can be destabilizing for some trainees. Nevertheless, it is my personal contention that trainees who find personal therapy overwhelmingly disturbing and difficult to a point where they withdraw from it or fail to attempt a meaningful exploration of their own unresolved issues, are not ready to deal effectively and safely with clients.

Undergoing personal therapy also allows students to experience what it is like to sit in the client's chair or to be on the other side of the couch. As a result of this 'being in the patient's shoes' they will therefore be better placed to empathize with the patient. This idea of better understanding the patient through understanding oneself is eloquently explained by Erich Fromm (1998: 100–1) within the context of the necessity for the analyst to be unafraid of his own unconscious:

*This leads me to what you might call the humanistic premise of my therapeutic work: There is nothing human which is alien to us. Everything is in me. I am a little child, I am a grown-up, I am a murderer, and I am a saint. I am narcissistic, and I am destructive. There is nothing in the patient which I do not have in me. And only inasmuch as I can muster within myself those experiences which the patient is telling me about, either explicitly or implicitly, only if they arouse and echo within myself can I know what the patient is talking about and can I give him back what he is really talking about . . .*

# A change for the better?

> *One knows another person only in as much as one has experienced the same. To be analyzed oneself means nothing else but to be open to the totality of human experience which is good and bad, which is everything . . . If I am analyzed that means . . . that I have made myself open, that there is a constant openness to all the irrationality within myself, and therefore I can understand my patient.*

The self-reflective process can be facilitated not just by personal therapy but also by the whole experience of training and the interaction with fellow trainees. By the very nature of therapy training courses, the ethos is one of self-questioning and self-monitoring. Merely being a part of such courses – assimilating theory, writing essays, engaging in clinical work, undergoing supervision, and all the other components of training – inevitably means that trainees soak up the process of self-exploration by a kind of osmosis. And, whether we seek it or not, change will come as surely as death and taxes.

My personal view in this whole debate about change within the context of training is that whilst it can be both beneficial and harmful in varying degrees, depending on the psychic state of the individual concerned, the desirability, indeed the necessity, for change of the kind that leads to insight and personal growth is beyond questioning. As to a more general rationale for self-exploration, I believe it can be summed up in the notion expressed by Socrates: 'The unexamined life is not worth living' (Plato 1997).

Philosophy can be valuable in illuminating the rationale for psychotherapeutic practice. It is therefore worth looking briefly at some philosophical concepts which underpin the idea that a life lived without self-exploration is the antithesis of what therapy and those who practice it should be. Let us turn first to Jean-Paul Sartre's ideas of choice and living in bad faith, as expounded by Carol Holmes (1998: 50 and 52), who contends that his ideas have 'important if not crucial ramifications for the therapeutic relationship and the ongoing therapeutic process':

> *The French philosopher Jean-Paul Sartre coined the term 'Bad Faith' to describe the human tendency for self-deception as a means of denying our subjective – and therefore true – experience in order that we should remain unaware of the conflicts that are often involved in the, albeit, limited choices that are always available to us . . . For the existentialists, bad faith (or self-deception) is an ongoing human conflict which makes us unwilling and intensely reluctant to engage honestly with ourselves and, by*

# On training to be a therapist

*extrapolation, ensures that we are also therefore unable to engage openly with others.*

Emmy van Deurzen-Smith (1997: 208–309) takes this theme a stage further by contrasting Sartre's ideas with those of Freud:

> *Freud argued that we have to keep certain things repressed in the unconscious because our consciousness cannot tolerate them . . . Sartre, of course, argued against the idea of repression by showing that the idea of a censor requires the process of decision making that requires a consciousness of sorts . . . Sartre preferred to speak of bad faith or self-deception. He considered 'repression' as an aspect of consciousness rather than relegating it to the dark unknown of an unconscious . . . What he put his finger on is the possibility that Freud's account is causally inverted . . . Instead of considering that something is repressed because it cannot be consciously faced, it may be that we simply prefer to describe those things as unconscious which we want to disclaim . . . Such avoidance can take the shape of actually moving away from things, or it can take the shape of denying that they are the case. In every instance, it involves a process of not facing up to what is, and it is this that is referred to as being in bad faith.*

Rollo May (1996: 40, original emphasis) examines the ideas of another great philosopher, Soren Kierkegaard, especially Kierkegaard's view of anxiety, in relation to therapy:

> *One basic aim of psychotherapy is to enlarge self-awareness by means of clarifying inner self-defeating conflicts which have existed because the individual has been forced to block self-awareness at earlier times. It is clear in therapy that these blockages in self-awareness have occurred because the person has been unable to move through accumulations of anxiety at various points in his growth. Kierkegaard makes it clear that selfhood depends upon the individual's capacity to* **confront anxiety and move ahead despite it.**

According to May, Kierkegaard's notion of anxiety is ultimately an optimistic one based on the potential for creativity, in other words the presence of anxiety within an individual indicates potentiality. There would, Kierkegaard says, be no anxiety if there were no possibility for creativity and change. May continues to elaborate on Kierkegaard's central theme (1996: 44) with a passage that epitomizes

## A change for the better?

the ongoing sense of angst and deconstruction versus growth and achievement that bedevils so many trainees and which, in essence, could be said to underpin the basic rationale for this book:

> It is valuable to let patients in therapy know this – to point out that the presence of anxiety means a conflict is going on, and so long as this is true, a constructive solution is possible. Now creating, actualizing one's possibilities, always involves destructive as well as constructive aspects. It always involves destroying the status quo, destroying old patterns within oneself, progressively destroying what one has clung to from childhood on, and creating new and original forms of living. If you do not do this you are refusing to grow, refusing to avail yourself of possibilities; you are shirking your responsibility to yourself.

For trainees suffering any or all of the traumas of training, especially the upheaval of personal change, the concepts expounded by May can be a powerful force for perseverance and stability. To end this chapter, however, it is the words of another great philosopher, Nietzsche (1976) that I have chosen to serve as an appropriate summation, or even a mantra for trainees: 'One must still have chaos in oneself to be able to give birth to a dancing star'.

# 3 The art of survival on the long and winding road

Not long before beginning work on this book, I remember reading a newspaper article about a notorious daredevil whose speciality was travelling round the world abseiling down tall buildings. He attracted the attention of the media in London when he performed his Spider Man act down the outside of The Tower at Canary Wharf, arguably the capital's most striking monument to yuppiedom, which rises up over the skyline of the Isle of Dogs like some bizarre smoked-glass spaceship.

Many of the people watching him plunge earthwards down the side of the 50-story building concluded that he was barking mad. Yet, peering through a glass darkly as he made his way down towards terra firma and the strong arm of the law, our abseiling 'madman' had, it appears, perceived the shape of true insanity. Having observed floor after floor of office workers clad in uncomfortable stifling suits, sitting in front of computer terminals like robots, looking as miserable as sin, he came up with a memorable remark along the lines of: 'They call me crazy, but looking at those guys inside those offices, I think I'm the only sane one round here'.

A couple of days after reading about this thought-provoking incident, I found myself seriously questioning my own sanity as I staggered through driving wind and rain on my way to the psychiatric hospital in the centre of London where I had an honorary placement

44

# The art of survival on the long and winding road

as part of my advanced training. Having dragged my unwilling body out of bed at the unspeakable hour of 5.30 am, an act of lunacy that, as a life member of the Late Risers Club, I would never remotely have dreamed of before I began my psychotherapy training, I asked myself what our abseiling philosopher would have made of my stoicism, or rather masochism.

The thought occurred that from the enjoyment point of view I would probably have been better employed taking a leaf out of his book – tying a length of elastic round my ankle, attaching it to a table leg, and attempting a bungee jump from the psychotherapy department on the seventh floor. Yet as I contemplated my state of shivering somnambulism through the streets of London, laughing at my galloping inanity, the phrase 'existential choice' sprang to mind.

The bottom line was that there was absolutely no element of coercion in my early morning misery. I had chosen to put myself through not only this demanding psychiatric placement, but also the whole gamut of training – essay writing, endless reading matter, clinical work, supervision, personal therapy and the various other requirements that go to make up the fine madness that constitutes the process of therapeutic apprenticeship. Furthermore, the whole caboodle was being shoehorned between work and family commitments in a seemingly impossible melange that often left me exhausted, dispirited and occasionally defeated. As the self-questioning reached manic proportions, the moans and the mutterings of colleagues came back to comfort me. In my hour of soul searching I remembered I was not alone.

How often do we hear fellow students of therapy questioning why they put themselves through years of pressure, personal deconstruction and psychic turmoil and pain, not to mention financial stress brought about by huge training fees and personal therapy, and the strain on relationships that can often reach crisis levels? Many are in the fortunate position of not having to work while they train, yet even they can find the process excessively demanding on occasions, and just like those who have to maintain a job in order to pay the fees, they also may question at times whether the end result is worth the angst involved in getting there.

In these circumstances the reaction can sometimes be to press the ejector seat button, and to indulge in the kind of self-destructive thinking that we so often encounter in our clients and which can be so hard to shift. As things appear to plummet from merely miserable to manic, we might begin thinking along the lines of 'That's it – I'm giving up. I'll never make a therapist. I'm useless – no, worse than useless. I'm probably doing the clients untold damage. My supervisor was right – how could I have made those moronic interpretations? A 6-year-old kid could have come up with something better. I'll just disappear quietly over the horizon and leave it to the experts.' Hyperbole, perhaps, but I am willing to bet that a good many readers will have found themselves, if not quite so ruthlessly self-annihilating, then at least undergoing a therapeutic crisis of confidence of some kind or another.

The quote from Stevenson, which I used in my introduction – 'To travel hopefully is a better thing than to arrive' – can seem a travesty when we are struck by acute training fatigue. Yet, as I indicated earlier, the element of choice is always present. One of my lecturers once remarked that sometimes the most therapeutic thing a client can do is to walk away from the therapy. We can choose not to continue our training at any time, and if we do continue, whether it be through gritted teeth or with a cheerful heart and a spring in our step, I believe that a kind of 'toughening up' process is an essential preparation for this line of work. It must never be forgotten that this 'impossible profession', as Nina Coltart called it (1992: 2), is not for the faint-hearted. To practice as a therapist requires mental resilience and a capacity to withstand attacks by patients, as well as uncertainty, unknowing and feelings of being de-skilled that affect not only trainees but even the most skilled practitioners, too.

Petrūska Clarkson (1999: 42) spells out the personal sacrifice that can be involved in this type of work when she writes:

> *Many have counted the cost in terms of the kind of emotional and physical exhaustion called 'burnout' – perhaps the result of lending the flame of one's own Physis for too long and too much to others . . . Psychotherapy is a vocation concerned with pathology, morbidity and disease . . . as well as growth, joy and exultation.*

The fraught and often painful odyssey that therapy training encompasses can sometimes seem more a test of survival than a learning process or an experience to be enjoyed for its own sake. Yet it is the ability to survive that is in fact a vital ingredient of that learning process, very much in the way we need to survive difficult encounters with clients. A therapist who can take a high degree of flak and constant attempts at undermining him or her, and can deal with it in a containing way is often exactly what clients, especially the more disturbed ones, require in order to survive themselves.

Survival is a major theme of Donald Winnicott's work. Talking of the more fragmented type of patient, he writes (1996: 279): 'Important from our point of view here is the idea of the survival of the analyst as a dynamic factor'. In looking at the difficulties of parents in dealing with adolescents, he says (1999: 145): 'Parents can only help a

# The art of survival on the long and winding road

little; the best they can do is to *survive*, to survive intact, and without changing colour, without relinquishment of any important principle'. Winnicott (1996: 285) also lists certain characteristics of the analytical setting, as originally postulated by Freud, among them:

> *The analyst would be reliably there, on time, alive, breathing . . . For the limited period of time prearranged (about an hour) the analyst would keep awake . . . In the analytic situation the analyst is much more reliable than people are in ordinary life, on the whole punctual, free from temper tantrums, free from compulsive falling in love, etc.*

These characteristics are part of the ability to survive whatever the client may bring, but as Jacobs (1995a: 84) points out in his book on Winnicott: 'Surviving is not the same as being passive. Not retaliating is different from not responding.'

From the point of view of therapy training, survival does entail arriving alive and punctually for sessions with clients, supervision and lectures on a consistent basis, although there is, of course, a lot more to it than simply turning up. Even when it feels like we are simply not comprehending and internalizing the basic concepts, and frustration and confusion begin to set in, it does not mean that learning and growth are not taking place – quite the opposite, in fact.

This is when the capacity to survive – sometimes feeling like dogged perseverance, sometimes more a masochistic refusal to lie down and concede defeat – begins to slip into gear. As we keep going tenaciously, the process of getting through the clinical work and the academic material gradually builds on itself in what is referred to as a spiral learning curve. So, clinical concepts that seem unfathomable at a relatively early stage in our training can suddenly click into place and become more real as our experience and understanding broadens and deepens. In the same way, books and theory that seemed as impenetrable as a crash course in quantum physics on first reading can appear contrastingly alive and meaningful when we return to them at a later stage.

Clarkson (1999: 20) covers this aspect admirably when she cites the case of a trainee, who reported:

> *When I first started learning psychotherapy it was like trying to learn a new language, say French, but when I saw an experienced psychotherapist working it appeared to me that she was speaking an entirely different language such as Chinese. The more I have learnt the more I have come to realise that she does indeed speak French, she just speaks it very well. And sometimes she speaks Chinese.*

## On training to be a therapist

In the fraught and arduous march of training, it is easy to feel dispirited and consumed by doubt, especially when we compare ourselves to supervisors, tutors and those with vastly more experience. But if we can hang on in there when everything seems so tenuous, those feelings of interminably treading water – and sometimes sinking – will slowly dissipate. As one by one the pieces begin to fit together, the realization of exactly how far we have come can begin to light the way ahead like the first fingers of dawn reaching out across the night sky. Then it becomes feasible to consider the very real possibility that even though there may still be a long way to go, we will eventually emerge as fluent French speakers, and may even become proficient at conversing in Chinese, too.

Not so fast, I hear some of you say, especially those only just beginning training, or more advanced students struggling with academic or clinical work – and with some justification. Before we can even think of speaking fluent French, let alone Cantonese, there are, as I have been at pains to indicate in this chapter and the preceding ones, ongoing battles to be fought and demons to be overcome. And, in order to make the journey as crisis-free and rewarding as is humanly possible, we need a strategy for survival, clearly defined goals, a personal commitment of faith and a rationale. This functions as the framework that contains us as trainee therapists, in the way the therapeutic frame does for our clients.

Stress is something that affects practitioners of all levels, but there are particular aspects of therapy training that can engender feelings of bewilderment and distress in students. In addition to my own observations regarding such matters as sibling rivalry, self-doubt, isolation, and personal change in Chapters 1 and 2, several other factors are highlighted by Delia Cushway (1997: 28), who has carried out extensive research into this area. Cushway offers one basic paradox of training:

> On the one hand, trainees are expected to become more self-aware and to expose their frailties as a step towards greater client sensitivity. On the other hand, they are selected because of their personal, as well as their academic, qualities and they therefore have to live up to this in training and display no weakness. Thus it is possible that, for some trainees, training may present seemingly unresolvable dilemmas.

Cushway then goes on (1997: 29) to provide details of her research into the most prevalent causes of stress in therapy trainees:

> In my own study of clinical trainees the most frequently reported stressors and percentage of trainees reporting each stressor were, in

## The art of survival on the long and winding road

*rank order: (1) poor supervision (37 per cent); (2) travelling (23 per cent); (3) deadlines (22 per cent); (4 =) lack of finance (19 per cent); (4 =) moving house (19 per cent); (6 =) separation from partner (17 per cent); (6 =) amount of academic work (17 per cent); (8) uncertainty about own capabilities (16 per cent); (9 =) too much to do (15 per cent); (9 =) changing placements (15 per cent) . . . When the stress questionnaire factor was analysed, six underlying factors were suggested by the analysis. These factors were named: (a) course structure and organisation; (b) workload; (c) poor supervision; (d) disruption of social support; (e) self-doubt; (f) client difficulties and distress.*

When several of these stress factors assail us at once the pressure can seem unbearable. Yet the commitment that will ultimately make us good and responsible therapists means that it can feel impossible to walk away from training and clients, even temporarily, when personal circumstances demand it. One student, Janet Higson, put it this way:

*Training is unrelenting. Once you start you cannot just decide to stop and have a break, principally because you have a responsibility to your clients. But what are you supposed to do when major life events like divorce or serious illness come along? It might sound almost trite, but there is something about wanting to do this work so badly that you carry on no matter what life throws at you. Or, as a friend of mine put it, you need to have a love affair with this work so that you do it in spite of everything.*

In attempting to look at ways of eliminating or minimizing stress levels, I do not consider it necessary or desirable to examine all the factors listed by Cushway and to prescribe specific antidotes to each. In any case, some of these issues, such as moving house, changing placements and being separated from partners, are by their nature peculiar to the individuals concerned, so any generalizations would be of little value. Having said that, there are, in my opinion, certain overall mechanisms and safeguards which can operate as a safety net or safety valve for most if not all of these stressors during training. One of these, supervision, and how to make best use of it will be covered in detail in Chapter 5.

Personal therapy, another crucial method of dissipating stress, was looked at in Chapter 2 when discussing the merits of self-exploration. Despite studies showing that therapy can destabilize trainee psychotherapists, I reiterate that I regard personal therapy as being beyond questioning for all therapy trainees. (More controversially, I believe it should also be mandatory in related fields of human interaction such as psychology and psychiatry.) In order to deal with the emotional angst and turmoil of others, we must surely have dealt to a greater or lesser degree with our own emotional issues.

Furthermore, if one looks at this whole issue from the point of view of the necessary survival of the therapist in the face of difficult or painful patient material, it would be almost impossible to imagine a therapist who found their own issues unbearable or overly destabilizing being able to manage a similar level of angst or disturbance in their clients. I believe we must also have experienced therapy from the inside in order to fully appreciate the process in its fullness. One of the benefits of this is learning by example or osmosis, as an 'apprentice' in any trade or profession does when honing his craft alongside someone far more experienced.

Although I believe personal therapy is the essential medium for self-exploration, it is by no means the total picture. Therapy can be maintained as an ongoing process or it can be the beginning of a journey of self-analysis and self-discovery that continues indefinitely with the individual seeking to understand themself, to accept their limitations, to work through psychic blocks and difficult issues, and to integrate the various sides of their character or personality. Besides personal therapy, this can be done in a variety of ways, which could include, for example, group therapy or co-counselling. Whatever route one takes, very few would disagree with the principle that some form of self-exploration is paramount for aspiring therapists, a line of thinking that is backed up by Freddie Strasser and John Karter, in a book on self-image (unpublished):

> ... it is well-established and accepted that clinicians before even thinking of helping others need to embark on their own self-explorations to get to know themselves as deeply as possible. It is regarded as a fundamental principle in all therapeutic orientations and establishments of psychotherapeutic education that the more you know yourself the better therapist you will be ... It is virtually impossible for therapists to understand others and listen accurately and empathically to them if they do not attempt to understand and accept their own vulnerabilities as well as their strengths.

Perhaps another, more focused way of looking at personal therapy as it applies to us in professional terms would be through the words of Thomas Carlyle. Referring to the famous exortation to 'Know Thyself' inscribed on the temple of Apollo at Delphi, Carlyle wrote of: 'The folly of that impossible precept, "Know Thyself"; till it be translated into this partially possible one, "Know what thou canst work at".'

## The art of survival on the long and winding road

As far as trainees are concerned, personal therapy is not only about knowing oneself better in order to become a more congruent, empathic and effective therapist. If we also look at personal therapy as an essential part of a 'self-help' system, it seems reasonable to state that, given a suitably competent and empathic therapist, personal therapy can offer trainees the kind of support that is needed through training. That is to say empathy and a meaningful exploration of issues, which may include an examination of anxiety, difficult feelings and trauma brought on by training matters as well as personal problems.

By a suitably competent and empathic therapist, I mean principally someone who is right for you as an individual. What is right for one person may be wholly unsuitable for someone else. It is certainly not just a matter of qualifications, orientation or professional reputation. There is an increasing consensus, backed up by research, that the relationship between therapist and patient is the overall key to therapeutic success (see Chapter 4), and that patients do not want a therapeutic automaton who operates through – perhaps that should be hides behind – rigidly programmed doctrine and dogma from which he or she finds it impossible to deviate.

Having a good support network of family and friends is, by and large, a desirable and beneficial situation for a trainee, but there are limits to the kind of empathy and the holding and containment they can offer. Family and friends are often not the best people to talk to about subjects that are difficult, painful, embarrassing or, in the case of training issues, too esoteric for them to comprehend fully. No matter how caring they are, they would find it virtually impossible to give us their undivided attention for 50 minutes, homing in on the more significant elements, in the way our therapists, with their carefully attuned therapeutic antennae, are able to do. This is a capacity Theodor Reik (1998), in his book of the same name, termed 'listening with the third ear'.

Dryden and Thorne (2000: 18), examining how to maximize the benefits of personal therapy for trainees, offer an interesting angle:

> Should trainees allow themselves full rein to discuss whatever they choose in their personal therapy or should the focus be on the experiences and implications of being a trainee? While the former is the norm, it is worth experimenting with the latter. This might be one way to boost the correlation between personal therapy and therapist effectiveness, for at present there is equivocal evidence that having personal therapy improves one's effectiveness as a counsellor or therapist.

Personally, I cannot see how one could talk about matters pertaining to training without bringing in issues from outside. However,

**51**

# On training to be a therapist

this suggestion has some merit in as much as there might well be a case for encouraging trainees to focus on training issues per se, as well as other matters, because issues specifically related to training can get neglected in the multiplicity of personal stuff that inevitably comes up week after week.

If we are looking for one good reason – perhaps that should be life-saving reason – for engaging in personal therapy as a safety valve, perhaps we could do worse than heed the words of Herbert Strean (1991: 9–10):

> *I believe that keeping quiet and listening has something to do with the high rate of heart attacks among analysts. They have to keep their anger, irritation, and sexual responses to themselves as they silently encourage the patient to express more fully his anger, irritation, and sexual wishes. The analyst is supposed to have no reaction when he is the recipient of intense love, hatred, dependency, sexuality . . . Perhaps if more analysts acknowledged their feelings to themselves, their incidence of heart attacks would be lower.*

Physical exercise, having fun, keeping up relationships with family members and friends, and generally maintaining a life and interests outside therapy are other ways of minimizing burn-out or stress-induced physical illness. The danger of becoming a therapy 'junkie' locked into the world of therapy to the exclusion of everything else, is highlighted by Anthony Storr (1995: 186):

> *There comes a point at which a certain kind of therapist may almost disappear as a definable individual, in rather the way that some self-sacrificing, Christian ladies become nonentities; people who are simply there for others, rather than existing in their own right. When psychotherapy is practised every day and all day, there is a danger of the therapist becoming a non-person; a prostitute parent whose children are not only all illegitimate, but more imaginary than real . . . living vicariously, through one's patients, is as much a danger for some psychotherapists as it is for some parents; and it is essential for the therapist to find some area in which he lives for himself alone, in which self-expression, rather than self-abnegation, is demanded.*

Taking breaks, whether for a holiday away or relaxation at home, is another vital component of therapeutic health in trainees and seasoned professionals. It was not until I attended a workshop on therapist burn-out at the Tavistock Clinic during my training that I realized

# The art of survival on the long and winding road

just how much effect clients can have on the psychological and physical well-being of therapists. This is in addition to the more obvious stressors such as suicidal clients and the potential threat of seriously disturbed clients making physical attacks on therapists.

Listening to many experienced therapists of all levels and orientations at the Tavistock event, I was struck by the repeated theme of being under psychological attack in an insidious and almost imperceptible way. Though we may not recognize the process as it is happening, clients, especially the more disturbed ones, can get under our psychic skins to the extent that their pathology is eating away at us like a cancer, often doing serious damage to our health, as the caveat from Strean above indicated so graphically.

Carl Goldberg (1993: 82) writes about the transferral of psychic pain from client to therapist. He is talking from a psychoanalytic perspective, but I believe his observations will have a meaning for therapists of many orientations:

> *Effective therapeutic work, from a psychoanalytic point of view, cannot be done unless the client transfers the resentments and hurts, including overwhelming rage experienced toward parental and other significant figures in the client's life, to the practitioner. The unconscious strategy of the client in this process is often to reverse the feelings of anger, helplessness and fright felt in the presence of a hurtful authority figure in the past by inducing the therapist to feel as frightened and helpless as the client did in the past.*

Holiday breaks are therefore essential in order to carry out a kind of psychic 'detoxifying' as well as to recharge one's batteries away from the constant drip, drip of harrowing material that one has to soak up on a daily basis. I say this as one who, as a trainee, found it extremely difficult to take breaks. Indeed, it was with some relief that I finally recognized I was in great danger of becoming the kind of 'non-person' Storr talks about above. At one point I resonated very much with an advertisement on television which showed a therapist listening with increasing strain to a series of clients throughout the day, then jumping into a taxi only to be 'assailed' by the cabby who also dumped all his problems in her lap. In my case, I would probably have felt obliged to give the poor fellow a free therapy session during my ride.

It is important to stress, however, that we should be careful not to idealize holiday breaks. The preparation and planning required, especially when children are involved, often compounded by frustrations engendered by delays in travelling and problems with accommodation, can lead to a feeling that the benefits are outweighed by the disadvantages.

# On training to be a therapist

The oppressive game of catch-up in work and domestic matters that is thrust on us as a result of going on vacation, can be another minus, as can the readjustment factor. Getting back to the daily grind and the realization that most of life is not about lying on sunny beaches sipping cool drinks, doing whatever you feel like doing when you feel like doing it, can bring you down to earth as dramatically as a botched landing.

Holiday breaks are a major source of anxiety in the specific context of ongoing therapy, and not just for the client, as we are constantly informed in our training, but for the therapist, too. Angst over holiday breaks can become overwhelming when we are trainees because of the all-consuming fear of losing clients. (Perhaps we should take heart from the fact that Freud took some patients on holiday with him.) When the nightmare becomes reality it can send our self-esteem plummeting and, allied to the more practical issue of lost hours, it can engender the feeling that it is impossible to allow oneself to take a break.

When we are preoccupied with the fear of a client leaving it can render us less effective as therapists because we may not be able to listen as effectively to what he is or she is trying to communicate. In the long run this may be picked up by the client, who could perceive us as lacking in empathy and decide to seek help elsewhere. In other words we will have brought about a self-fulfilling prophecy, a scenario that is discussed by Abrahao Brafman (1999: 21):

> Once you set qualification as your goal, every mishap feels like a catastrophic, inescapable failure. You can get to a point where if your patient misses one session, you become fearful that another period of weeks (months?) will be lost before you find a new training case. This is dangerous, as you can find yourself treating the patient with the awful mixture of placation and resentment that we have towards a person felt to have 'power' over us.

The opportunity to take a step back from therapeutic situations can be beneficial for the therapist, not just because it can offer relief from stress, but also in terms of being able to re-evaluate and rethink the work and therefore to be in a position to offer better and more effective therapy to the patient. It must also be said that therapy does not stop during breaks, indeed some of the most significant work can be done *in absentia*, as it is between sessions when the work is not disrupted by a break.

Self-monitoring and self-preservation aside, I believe there are two more fundamental issues that need to be seriously considered by trainees in terms of making it through training to a place of therapeutic

## The art of survival on the long and winding road

maturity and security where we are sure we really want work to professionally in this field and are thus in a position to get the most out of our ensuing careers as therapists. The first of these – developing a sense of what exactly one is trying to achieve as a therapist – is a huge, complex and divisive issue, which has been written about and debated at enormous length. I make no excuse for merely touching on it in the briefest way here in order that students should at least be aware of the need to take time to think it through properly and become aware of their limitations and the limitations of therapy generally.

The objectives of therapy differ in varying degrees according to which of the ever-increasing schools of psychotherapy and counselling you espouse. I will take three major therapeutic schools, client centred, psychodynamic and existential, as contrasting examples, and hope that exponents/devotees of other approaches will not feel too slighted given the obvious limitations on space.

Carl Rogers, founding father of the client centred approach, looked to what has been described as an almost naïvely optimistic view of the human capacity for self-induced growth, although he strongly rebuffed the criticism that he adopted a 'Pollyanna' style view of therapeutic change. Given the appropriate or 'core' therapeutic conditions – empathy, congruence and unconditional positive regard – Rogers (1998: 26–37, original emphasis) said that clients have a natural tendency to move towards a state of psychic well being or wholeness:

*It is has been my experience that persons have a basically positive direction* ... *When I can sensitively understand the feelings which they are expressing, when I am able to accept them as separate persons in their own right, then I find that they tend to move in certain directions. And what are these directions in which they tend to move? The words which I believe are most truly descriptive are words such as positive, constructive, moving towards self-actualization, growing towards maturity, growing towards socialization. I have come to feel that the more fully the individual is understood and accepted, the more he tends to drop the false fronts with which he has been meeting life, and the more he tends to move in a direction which is forward.*

Rogers summed up the essence of this therapeutic nirvana by offering four criteria for the emerging person (1998: 115). These are 'openness to experience', which needs little elaboration; 'trust in one's organism', that is to say one's own organism is felt as 'a suitable instrument for discovering the most satisfying behaviour in each immediate situation'; developing 'an internal locus of evaluation', as opposed to

# On training to be a therapist

needing validation from others; and 'willingness to be a process', that is the individual comes to understand that he is 'not a fixed entity, but a process of becoming'.

The Rogerian ideals are in marked contrast to those of the psychodynamic approach, which has its roots in the psychoanalytic theory of Sigmund Freud, who saw the goal and the journey to that goal in a decidedly greyer hue. Freud regarded human growth towards wholeness as a matter of balancing various primitive drives, principally sexuality (libido), self-preservation and the death instinct. He saw the young human as having to negotiate various stages of what he regarded as libidinal development, the oral, anal, phallic-oedipal and latency phases, or risk being stuck at that particular phase of development and thus experience varying degrees of psychic malfunctioning.

Another key element in Freud's theories was bringing repressed material – emotions, feelings, and memories that have been banished from consciousness because they are too painful to acknowledge – into the conscious area of the mind and in so doing to eliminate the neuroses created by the repression. However, it is the recognition and working through of so-called transference phenomena – displaced views of the therapist as a figure from the client's past – that has always been the linchpin of psychoanalysis and is still a fundamental component of the modern psychodynamic approach. These so-called 'transference neuroses' (which can be located in the various stages of libidinal development) must be resolved, that is worked through and seen for the distorting influence that they have on the client's current relationships, in order for the client to function in a well-rounded way.

Melanie Klein and other theorists of what is known as the object-relations school of psychoanalysis eschew Freudian drive theory in favour of an infant's relationship to its objects, i.e. significant others. They maintain, *inter alia*, that there will be a similar price to pay in terms of neurosis and psychopathology in later life if there is a failure to move from the paranoid-schizoid position – where the child indulges in splitting his objects into good and bad with no in-between – to the depressive position, where good and bad are seen as residing in the object at the same time. Klein suggested that the origins of neurosis lay in the first year of life rather than the first few years and she was very much concerned with highlighting and interpreting what she viewed as the infant's vivid and aggressive phantasy life.

The theories of Donald Winnicott, another pioneering figure of the psychoanalytic movement, offered a further variant on the classical approach. Winnicott's view of the origins of psychic difficulties very much centred on the infant's response to its mother and how the mother meets those responses. The right connection between what Winnicott referred to as a 'good enough' mother (1960: 591) and her infant leads to the development of a true self, as opposed to a false self. The development of a false self can also be the result of painful or difficult external stimuli in later life. Winnicott focused on the individual's difficulties with the environment and how failures of the environment to meet their needs shaped their character, rather than a preoccupation with drives and instincts and the various stages of childhood as postulated by Freud.

In essence, psychodynamic therapy, as it has evolved from psychoanalysis, centres around the resolution of certain key conflicts of an internal nature, which will, in theory, allow healthy development to ensue, as well as the bringing to consciousness of repressed material that is causing neurotic unhappiness. The psychodynamic view of success in therapy rests very much on the individual knowing the 'why' of their current mental state rather than the 'how' and the 'what', which is favoured by the existential approach. Putting it another way, insight and awareness followed by integration and acceptance leads to freedom to be oneself by throwing off the shackles of intrapsychic impediments and thus being a more complete person.

The existential approach does not place emphasis on internal or intrapsychic concerns. It focuses on external phenomena and the individual's way of relating to those phenomena, known as his 'being-in-the-world'. Achieving a personally gratifying way of being-in-the-world begins from the standpoint that we are all 'thrown into' the world and have to try to make meaning from what is essentially a meaningless situation before being thrown summarily out of the world at the end of our lives. If one wanted to take a facetious view of this approach, it could be summed up by the slogan seen on tee-shirts, which states: 'Life is a bitch, then you die'.

Translated into therapeutic goals, the existential approach is not so much about an end product as an acceptance of one's being-in-the-world. This is summed up by Emmy van Deurzen-Smith (1997: 21):

> *The aim of existential counselling is to clarify, reflect upon and understand life. Problems in living are confronted and life's possibilities and boundaries are explored. Existential counselling does not set out to cure people in the tradition of the medical model. Clients are not considered to be ill but sick of life or clumsy at living. Existential counselling does not set out to change people either, as in the tradition of behavioural science. It does not assume that people necessarily need to change or that they are willing or able to change. The assistance provided is aimed at finding direction in life by gaining insight into its workings . . . The focus therefore is on life itself, rather than one's own personality.*

# On training to be a therapist

The notion of 'cure', which is rejected by van Deurzen-Smith, would be treated suspiciously if not antagonistically by therapists of most approaches, yet it is something that bedevils many trainees (and experienced practitioners, too), who are desperate to demonstrate tangible results. In the search for what one might reasonably attempt to achieve in therapy, let us turn first to the words of Neville Symington. Looking at the issue of what he terms 'the autonomy of the self', Symington writes (1996: 177):

> The question revolves around this point: what is the aim of therapy? Does it aim to make me feel good and whole, or is it to equip me to manage the crises of my life? To this question, there follows another. What ultimately is it that strengthens the self, that enables the self to ride the emotional storms? What factor is it in the self that raises self-esteem? Jung (1933, p270) said: 'The patient does not feel himself accepted unless the very worst of him is accepted, too.' All aspects of the self need to be accepted: the loving and the hating, the good and the bad, the admired and the despised.

As an understated and unpretentious summation of the limitations of therapeutic endeavour, there is much to commend Christopher Badcock's distillation of what Freud regarded as the aims of psychoanalytic therapy. Discussing the implications of Freud's social theory and the need to allow frustration of one's id (i.e. one's instinctual or primitive self) in the interests of the need of one's ego to live in a community, Badcock (1993: 148) said Freud's view of the fundamental aim of therapy was 'to replace unconsciously motivated, irrational neurotic misery with ordinary human unhappiness'.

Brown and Pedder (1994; 200) take a different line on Freudian ideals:

> Where do we hope we have got after more extensive psychotherapy? Freud defined mental health as the capacity to find satisfaction in work and love. Perhaps we should add a capacity for play, or, in other words, define health as the ability to find satisfaction in work, play and loving relationships. If this sounds rather ideal, it is less so than the definition adopted by the World Health Organization in its Charter that 'health is a state of complete physical, mental and social well-being'! Such magical solutions psychotherapy cannot provide, but at best it can help launch people in the direction of greater freedom and growth.

The trouble with concepts like 'freedom' and 'growth', and the Rogerian ideals, is that they are not only vague and open to a

## The art of survival on the long and winding road

myriad of interpretations, but they can also carry implicit value judgements. In a similar way the concept of client autonomy, which is often cited as the principal basis for therapeutic change, can be questioned, as indeed it is by Edward Erwin (1997: 28, original emphasis):

> . . . autonomy is often recommended as the main, if not the only, legitimate goal of psychotherapy. What are the arguments for this position? One runs like this. There are no objective values, or at least none that can be established as correct. Consequently, the therapist should increase the client's autonomy so that he or she can better make his or her own value decisions. The argument is incoherent. The therapist accepts a certain evaluative assumption: that if there are no objectively true value judgements, then autonomy **should** be the main goal. The therapist then tries to defend **this** value judgement on the grounds that no value judgement, including his or her own, is true (or false), or at least is known to be true.

Erwin continues (1997: 29):

> The main objection to making autonomy the main goal is that quite often this is not what the client wants. In some such cases, the client is confused about his own welfare, and it may be reasonable for the therapist to use rational persuasion to convince him of the value of a certain therapeutic outcome. Not all cases, however, are like this.

If one were to take a philosophical viewpoint, the goal of happiness, as defined by Bertrand Russell (2000: 191), might offer a reasonable basis for what therapy might aim at:

> All unhappiness depends upon some kind of disintegration or lack of integration; there is disintegration within the self through lack of coordination between the conscious and the unconscious mind; there is lack of integration between the self and society where the two are not knit together by the force of objective interests and affections. The happy man is the man who does not suffer from either of these failures of unity, whose personality is neither divided against itself nor pitted against the world. Such a man feels himself a citizen of the universe, enjoying freely the spectacle that it offers and the joys it affords, untroubled by the thought of death because he feels himself not really separate from those who will come after him. It is in such profound instinctive union with the stream of life that the greatest joy is to be found.

## On training to be a therapist

Yet even the seemingly indisputable notion of happiness can be questioned in therapeutic terms. Roger Bentall, writing in the *Journal of Medical Ethics* (1992: 94–8), devotes a whole paper to the proposition that happiness is evidence of severe mental disturbance. In the paper entitled 'A proposal to classify happiness as a psychiatric disorder', Bentall summarizes his claim by suggesting that the term 'happiness' be replaced by the more formal description 'major affective disorder, pleasant type'. One can assume that his claim is not meant to be taken 100 per cent seriously, but, as detailed in his summary, it offers interesting food for thought:

> *I have argued that happiness meets all reasonable criteria for a psychiatric disorder. It is statistically abnormal, consists of a discreet cluster of symptoms, there is at least some evidence that it reflects the abnormal functioning of the central nervous system, and it is associated with various cognitive abnormalities – in particular, a lack of contact with reality. Acceptance of these arguments leads to the obvious conclusion that happiness should be included in future taxonomies of mental illness, probably as a form of affective disorder.*

As I have indicated, the aim of this whistle-stop tour of therapeutic goals was not to offer an overview that could in any way be regarded as comprehensive, rather to stimulate reflection and thought as to our own aspirations and hopes within the therapeutic framework. This line of self-questioning links to my suggestion in Chapter 1 that we should carefully examine our motives for working as therapists. What I will say in summary regarding our aims and ideals of therapy is that these should be both considered and realistic. Thus, if we are going into the profession with an intent to cure in the medical sense we are not only in the grip of a serious delusion, we are probably in danger of doing ourselves and, more importantly, our clients, more harm than good. And taking this a step further, if the aim is to change people to our own way of being and doing, or to live vicariously through our clients, or, worse still, to wield a kind of power that one is not able to wield outside the consulting room, then quite simply it is better to walk way from training.

As a direct corollary to thinking through our aims and goals in therapy, the question of whether we genuinely believe therapy works is at least as vital to establishing a proper rationale for training as having therapeutic goals, and thus entering the profession for the right reasons. It is easy to become lost in the cosy world of therapy and not only to fail to address our own doubts about the efficacy of the therapeutic process, but to ignore the views of the outside world as well. The

# The art of survival on the long and winding road

public perception of therapy and therapists is far from universally sympathetic even in this so-called enlightened age, the attitude of those outside the profession often ranging from the slightly cynical and sniggering to open hostility.

The main obstacle to rebutting those attacks is a lack of any really consistent data to support a case for the defence. There are studies that appear to reinforce the value of therapy, but equally there are those that show no such benefits. The problem is that therapy is not a science in the way medicine is and as such there is a welter of evidence, albeit circumstantial, for the prosecution.

Take for example the words of Lewis Wolberg in his comprehensive two-volume work on the principles and practice of psychotherapy (1988: 81): 'In some circles the idea still prevails that psychotherapy is a swamp of marshy theories embedded in a quagmire of metapsychological slogans and convoluted methodologies.'

Wolberg goes on to mount a defence of psychotherapy, which is at best equivocal, by stating (1988: 101–102):

> *Even if we accept what the most dubious researchers now concede, that psychotherapy is at least minimally effective and better than no treatment or the use of a placebo, most impartial observers would have to consider it a beneficial enterprise . . . But can we say it is cost-effective and that the benefits justify the expenditure of time, effort and money?*

Some have far stronger and more destructive words for the process, notably Jeffrey Masson, whose book, *Against Therapy* (1997), is one long tirade against the profession, and might seem, to objective observers, to blow a gaping hole in the credibility of therapy generally. Mike Lawson, vice-chairman of the mental health organization MIND is quoted on the cover of Masson's book as labelling it 'A brilliant and courageous exposé of the damage that unavoidably occurs in the name of "psychotherapy"'.

Masson's viewpoint seems biased to the point of absurdity in that he appears to seek out only high-profile cases of abuse by therapists (he would doubtless claim that many lower profile cases go unreported), but whatever your view of his broadside, he does highlight the potential risks of abuse of power and psychological manipulation in a powerful way.

The problem with Masson and others like him is that they are preoccupied with negative experiences and case histories, and make little or no attempt to offer a balanced view. It is always easy to single out examples of abuse and unprofessional conduct in any line of work,

## On training to be a therapist

whether it be psychotherapy, medicine, religion or the law, and to 'hype' these at the expense of the thousands of honest, well-meaning professionals who would never become involved in client abuse or malpractice. This is very much the line taken by newspapers when they parade banner headlines about therapists seducing clients or vicars running off with parishioners' wives. To write about the overwhelming majority of therapists who do *not* seduce their clients or vicars who do *not* run off with other people's wives would simply not sell newspapers.

In view of the sustained attacks on the 'unscientific' nature of psychotherapy, there is a preoccupation with trying to appease the critics and to offer proper research-based evidence. From a client's point of view this is highly laudable in that any monitoring and questioning of therapy practice goes some way towards offering a kind of quality assurance for consumers. I am aware that practitioners of models such as cognitive behavioural therapy will not agree, but I believe that the essence of therapy is bringing about change through a uniquely interpersonal process, not one that can or should be reduced to yet another formulaic branch of science. To become obsessed with the whole evidentiary syndrome at the expense of this interpersonal element can negate that essence.

There are far wider implications for therapy in this increasing demand for evidence and results. These are highlighted in an article by John McLeod in the BACP's journal *Counselling and Psychotherapy Research* (2001: 116). Examining what he terms a crisis for practitioners of psychotherapy and counselling in the United States of America due to insistence by medical insurance companies on paying only for scientifically-based therapies, McLeod says:

> *It is as though the purchasers of therapy are saying that now, after 50 years of research, the profession should know what works and what does not, and that they are willing to pay only for therapy that is empirically proven and quality-controlled. But from the practitioner perspective, the direction in which the 'psychotherapy industry' appears to be heading is deeply worrying: erosion of professional autonomy, status and payment levels, and a pervasive sense that what is being offered is not what many clients need.*

In a world that mistakenly and worryingly equates science with omniscience, it is becoming increasingly hard to convince outsiders that the 'unknowing', explorative, relationship-based process of psychotherapy is justifiable, a situation that is as disturbing as it is misguided. David Smail (1978: 59) aptly sums up the futility of attempting to turn psychotherapy into scientism:

# The art of survival on the long and winding road

*Countless authorities can be cited for any particular view, count-
less hypotheses can be advanced to account for any set of data,
countless errors of research design and statistical analysis can be
advanced to destroy opponents' claims. Somewhere underlying this
endless and singularly fruitless process is the myth of the 'crucial
experiment': the belief that one day a study will be carried out of
such perfect design, such faultless mathematical precision, such
impeccable logic and such compelling empirical content as to silence all critics, who will instead be forced into mute reverence for
the therapeutic truths revealed.*

The problem for trainees who are seeking to justify the
profession to themselves and to others is that whilst therapy is a joint
venture in which client and therapist are partners in a process of exploration, *we* are often the ones groping in the dark, and it is all too easy to
pathologize the 'stuckness' or the wish to quit therapy and throw it back
on the client. The situation can be experienced in reverse in our own
therapy where there can be times when we seem to be going nowhere
fast and paying through the nose for the privilege.

When doubts set in and there seems little in the way of a
lifeline to be grasped, there is much to be said for focusing determinedly
on the positive experiences and retaining them as a buffer against future
doubt and insecurity. As an example, I vividly remember the response of
my supervisor in my first placement, at a university, when a fellow
supervisee expressed feelings of dread and uselessness after her client, a
seriously distressed and potentially suicidal young student, failed to return for further therapy after the initial session. 'We will never know
the outcome', my supervisor said. 'And that is something we have to
live with as therapists. But it might well be that your one session with
that client saved his life.'

Those words were repeated almost exactly to me at a social
gathering not long afterwards, only this time the sentiment came from
someone who had undergone extensive therapy. Having become only
too familiar with and wary of the kind of mocking or cynical responses
you frequently receive when you own up to training for this curious
profession, I was instinctively on my guard when a lady, to whom I had
only recently been introduced, asked me what I did for a living. With
my usual dose of self-parody I replied: 'Oh, I'm one of those – a psychotherapist'. Becoming visibly serious, she said: 'I'd never criticize psychotherapy. When I was at an all-time low point, a psychotherapist saved
my life'.

The essence of everything I believed about therapy was
encapsulated in and validated in that moment; the doubts I had harboured

were put into perspective by that very real and most moving testimony. I know a colleague who had a similar life-saving affirmation from a long-term client when he ended therapy with emotional and heartfelt thanks to her for deliverance from his demons. I am not saying that these life or death transformations are the rule – we cannot work miracles and sometimes we cannot help at all. But psychotherapy *can* make a difference and often it is a difference of life-changing significance for the patient, if only to clear away confusion and help a seed of self-help to germinate.

As John Rowan put it (1992: 166), in response to Katherine Mair's assertion that psychotherapists exploit the mystique of the expert healer:

> *Psychotherapy can abandon all its false pretensions and still be of use to people in need. People can be served best by being encouraged to have less faith in experts and more in themselves. And this is just what happens when psychotherapy is successful.*

As a clergyman once said to me when talking of people going through a crisis of faith, there is nothing wrong with honest doubt, a sentiment that applies equally to the practice of therapy. Indeed, it would be wrong not to question and to go on questioning what we are doing long after we have qualified. Continued soul searching and the rejection of even the slightest hint of complacency can only be good for us and even more beneficial for our clients. In this context and in summary, I return to my introduction where I used the image of therapy training being akin to learning to drive a car. Perhaps we should never think of relinquishing our L-plates, but keep them next to us in the car instead as a constant reminder of the perennial struggle on the long and winding road.

# 4    The dangers in playing it by the book

As well as being one of England's most flamboyant prime ministers, Benjamin Disraeli appears to have been something of a philosopher. Disraeli succinctly verbalized a seminal concept for anyone aspiring to work in the field of psychotherapy when he said: 'Experience is the child of Thought, and Thought is the child of Action. *We cannot learn men from books'*.

Students of psychotherapy struggling to master theoretical concepts, and even those who are not unduly fazed by the academic demands of training, might do well to write out the last sentence of Disraeli's quote and keep it somewhere readily accessible as a perman-ent reminder of this crucial principle. For no matter how intellectually accomplished and bookish one happens to be, such knowledge can never – indeed *should* never – be a substitute for an instinctive and/or experientially-gained understanding of people and an ability to empathize with them.

The problem is that books can be seriously addictive, espe-cially when we are trainees, with a voracious appetite for learning and a sponge-like capacity for absorbing theory. Those seductive covers with their cleverly-crafted blurbs offer promises of omniscience, empower-ment, academic validation and so much more. That is why browsing specialist bookshops or the therapy sections of the major bookstores can be a financial minefield for those of us who are trigger happy with our credit cards.

## On training to be a therapist

Taking this a step further, it is all too easy to fall into the trap of seeing books as the keys to the therapeutic kingdom, and theory as the tool that will unlock the timeless mystery of therapy. As a result, we can become overwhelmed by tutors firing off endless book titles and academic papers at us, and can end up feeling like little children given free rein in a sweet shop and not knowing which of the goodies to grab first. The point is that tutors are expected to demonstrate an ability to trawl the therapeutic literature almost at will, but that does not mean that we as students are required to emulate them – unless we have aspirations to teach – or that reading every last work on therapy will necessarily make us better therapists.

I have never forgotten an off-the-cuff piece of advice from our seminar leader on my foundation course. Talking in general terms about books on psychotherapy and counselling, he said something along the lines of: 'Never get hung up on any particular book or books, just dip into them. Books are just one element of your training. Don't try to understand everything you read. Pick out the bits that seem relevant to you personally.'

As I had just begun training and was in the process of trying to wade through Bion's *Experiences in Groups* (1996), which despite its reputation as one of the great works of psychotherapeutic literature seemed to me to be written in colloquial Sanskrit, those words were received like manna from heaven. Thereafter, whenever I found myself being overwhelmed by the seemingly impenetrable writings of yet another theorist, my seminar leader, with his memorable phrase, 'just dip into them', sprang to my rescue like a kind of psychic superman.

When we are in training there are, of course, the very real demands of academic assessment to be considered. Yet, as we sit surrounded by piles of unread tomes and photocopies of seminal papers by great names from the pantheon of psychotherapy, an insidious process can develop. In our wish to seem competent, professional and, on occasions, omniscient, we can become slaves to theory to the detriment of our practice.

Whilst theory is a crucial element in our understanding and mastery of therapeutic practice, it should arguably be seen as one of the many components in our armoury, not the wherewithal. In other words, theory should be seen as an adjunct to practice, not the primary motivating force. We need theory to illuminate our understanding of psychic processes in our clients, but it should be seen as a base from which to evolve our own style, otherwise it will stifle our creative potential in the therapeutic encounter. One could compare the rationale for developing a basic theoretical framework in therapy to the need for professional sportsmen, such as tennis players and golfers, to learn the

## The dangers in playing it by the book

basic techniques of strokeplay before evolving their own, sometimes idiosyncratic way of playing the game, which allows room for their own creativity and unique talent to flower.

Joyce McDougall (1986: 23) sums up the limitations of theory:

> *A preoccupation with theory could only obscure what the analyst is trying to discern of the latent communication behind each patient's analytic discourse. Although what we hear is immeasurably enlarged by all we have learned, and may still learn, from different theoreticians, such learning enriches our clinical work only to the extent that the theories have become an intimate part of our own analytical experience – not only the experience of personal analysis and the confirmation that clinical practice brings, but also the continuing self-analysis in which all analysts must engage. Without the enrichment of self-knowledge, theory is an impediment rather than an aid to what we hear. It may block the emergence of new hypotheses about the psychic reality of, and our specific reactions to, each of our patients.*

What is often forgotten is that theory, like science, is not holy writ; it is a postulation by an individual of what he or she believes to be the ultimate truth – and will only remain as such until the next theory comes along to challenge and either usurp or invalidate that belief or viewpoint. In this respect it is useful to ponder the *Oxford Dictionary* definitions of the word 'theory', which read as follows: '1. A supposition or system of ideas explaining something . . . 2. A speculative (esp. fanciful) view . . . 3. The sphere of abstract knowledge or speculative thought.' These definitions show theory for what it very often is, namely the stuff of speculation and supposition, not proven beyond doubt or unchallengeable. This should offer some comfort, and perhaps a caveat, too, for psychotherapy and counselling trainees who can tend to see theory and theoreticians in an overwhelmingly important, or superego-ish way.

Being obsessively bookish can be a defence against feeling inadequate. After all, who can blame us if we home in on any form of relief from the regressive sense of being judged, scrutinized, and striving desperately to prove our worth, a feeling that echoes our days as schoolchildren when we were overawed by seemingly all-knowing, all-powerful teachers. That is how it can feel when we are in training, which is why theory and books can seem a safe-haven offering a welcome buffer against the demands of clients, supervisors and tutors. Adam Phillips highlights another negative aspect of theory, based on Freudian concepts, which might resonate with trainees in terms of their relationships with their

**67**

# On training to be a therapist

peers. Writing about children's fantasies arising from the birth of a sibling, Phillips says (1999: 19):

> *Often stimulated, as Freud frequently points out, by the birth of a sibling – and other people, of course were beginning to participate in Freud's psychoanalysis as both colleagues and rivals – these fantasies, whether they be sexual theories or the more disguised and sophisticated family romances, were the medium for the child's struggle for psychic survival; the child's attempts, however forlorn, to refind a place in the world. Theory, Freud intimates, is intrinsically rivalrous; it is about being better placed than somebody else.*

As I indicated in Chapter 1, the whole ethos of training can be said to engender competitiveness in varying degrees. And, if we are honest, there is much satisfaction, not to mention kudos, in the occasional piece of academic name dropping. Letting slip casually that we just happen to have finished reading the entire works of Freud or that we trolled through Bowlby's trilogy, *Attachment, Separation and Loss* (1991), over the weekend can work wonders for a sagging ego, not to mention the Brownie points to be acquired from course leaders.

In my Introduction, I mentioned that when I began work as a journalist for the new broadsheet newspaper, *The Independent*, Andreas Whittam Smith, the editor, told us to be careful not to make the mistake of writing for other journalists rather than for the paper's readers. I believe this happens with depressing regularity in therapeutic literature – especially in the psychoanalytic field – where the wish to be seen as frightfully clever and intellectually pioneering often results in authors producing material that is designed to impress and dazzle rather than inform and edify.

If we can look at books in a more critical, objective way, instead of allowing ourselves to be coerced into a 'king's new clothes' mentality where it feels wrong to question what is before our eyes, it can help us to get more out of reading and theory. I believe we can get maximum benefit from theoretical concepts if we take from them and integrate what we personally find relevant and compatible with our own experience and core values. This in turn is about developing the ability to be 'real' in our work as therapists, as opposed to adopting a therapeutic 'false self' because it seems correct or expedient to do so.

I will elaborate on this crucially important area later in the chapter, but before doing so it seems pertinent to examine what represents a major hurdle for many students in their continuing efforts to come to terms with theory as a part of training, and indeed practice, namely the seemingly overwhelming and oppressive business of essay

# The dangers in playing it by the book

writing and case studies. Putting pen to paper, or nowadays fingers to keyboard, surfaced time and again in answers to my student questionnaires as a major worry and source of angst. Indeed, it would be no exaggeration to say that for many trainees, essay writing appears to induce a higher incidence of sleepless nights and nightmarish scenarios than clinical encounters with the most complex and difficult clients.

For some it can even be terminal as far as their ability to get through the course is concerned. For example, I happened to come across an extreme example of 'negative essay syndrome' in a very personal way, through an encounter that taught me never to judge a book by its cover – or a woman by her duster. There is nothing sexist intended in that last remark because the truth of this concept was brought home to me in the most humbling manner by a lady I once employed as a cleaner. Aged 40 and a single mother of four children, she came from a working-class background and had little in the way of formal education. She had left school at 15 and worked her way through a succession of menial jobs, eventually settling on domestic cleaning as a reliable, reasonably well-paid source of income.

It did not take too long before I found myself receiving an object lesson in the dangers of superficial judgement and the way in which our preconceptions can cut us off from what may prove to be valuable and edifying interactions. As we got to know each other better, my cleaning lady, who, for the purposes of this book, I will call Ann, showed herself to be singularly insightful and empathic in the whole area of relationships, emotions and human conflict. I very soon realized I had employed someone whose ability to sort out other people's trash and deal with their chaos extended to matters internal as well as external.

One day Ann told me she had noticed the books on psychotherapy and counselling in my study, and when I explained about my work and my training in that field she informed me that she had been in training to become a counsellor, but had been forced to give it up. Due to her lack of formal education and her inability to spell and write gramatically, she told me she was unable to complete the essays demanded by her course in a way that would have satisfied the adjudicators. I believe there was also an issue of self-esteem and lack of self-belief, inasmuch as she held a sedimented view of herself as intellectually inferior to her peers.

Despite my attempts to encourage her to talk the whole thing through with her college, or to take a different, more practically-based course, she was adamant that there was no going back. What a tragedy, I thought. Here was a woman who would have made a superb therapist, but because of her circumstances she would never be able to use her natural talent for relating and empathizing. The many potential

# On training to be a therapist

clients who would undoubtedly have benefitted from her perceptiveness and skills had been thwarted by a singularly cruel variation of writer's block.

It is the more familiar form of writer's block that causes such fear and paralysis for many students of therapy. The process of essay writing can also evoke resentment and despair, and it can infantilize individuals who are otherwise notably focused and self-possessed. It could be argued that the ability to write essays should play little or no part in the assessment of an individual for qualification as a therapist, as my little vignette above appears to underline. Adjudication could be based on clinical work, supervisors' reports and the personal qualities of the trainee, that is to say the perception of his or her ability to be with the client in an empathic and therapeutic way.

One trainee, Riann Croft, offers a traumatic but by no means untypical experience of essay writing:

> I failed all my essays and case studies on my diploma course and wasn't given any written feedback as to why I'd failed or how I could re-write them. I found this devastating and it took me until the following year to re-write them. On my supervision course, I've had a lot of help getting to grips with the written work, but the shadow of those failed essays has caused me a lot more pain and anguish than I would have believed possible: I've had panic attacks and felt very weepy and hopeless.

Another trainee, Peter Harris, succinctly summed up the feelings of many: 'There are too many essays. I have no idea why essay writing is considered a measure of ability to be a good therapist.'

Whether we like it or not, essays *are* a part of training courses, and a personal view is that on balance they should be one of the criteria for assessment. When we are training as therapists it is important to be able to explain what we are trying to do and why we are doing it in a way that is considered and coherent. As I said earlier, the understanding and internalizing of basic theoretical concepts gives us an essential platform from which to build our own individual style or approach. Furthermore, it can be argued that the discipline of getting all of this down on paper goes some way towards showing our commitment to the overall process of training, and thus of therapy itself.

That is no help to those suffering from negative essay syndrome, or what might be better termed MESS – manic essay survival syndrome. There are those lucky souls who sail through essays without being affected but they are clearly in the minority. An MA student at the college I was attending compared the feeling you get before beginning a

# The dangers in playing it by the book

dissertation to the sensation a mountaineer must feel looking up from ground level to the summit of Everest. Whilst essays and case studies are arguably less demanding than dissertations, many fellow students I encountered during my own training seemed to approach them with as much relish as they would having to climb the north face of the Eiger without crampons.

There was an assumption amongst many of my peers that because I had been a journalist I found essay writing enviably simple, but this was as ill-founded as it was annoying. Essay writing filled me with as much dread as anyone, and yet there was one simple truth contained in the familiar charge of 'It's all right for you.You're used to this kind of thing'. The fact is that for many students the basic difficulty stems from lack of practice. Many have never written anything more demanding than a 'thank you' letter since they left school or university. When the time comes to dredge the depths of their mental resources for techniques that might once have seemed second nature, the mind-set that carried them through year upon year of study and examinations appears to have gone beyond recall.

The fact that we are faced with having to carry out what is often our first practical academic task or tasks since leaving full-time education can have a regressive effect. Memories of unfinished compositions, trotting out woefully transparent excuses to teachers, and writing out 500 times 'I must hand my essays in on time' can come flooding back as we ponder the written demands of training courses that somehow we chose to put to the back of the mind when we signed up for the course in the first place.

I used the word 'paralysis' earlier on for the simple reason that the mere thought of beginning a piece of written work can induce a state of frozenness. Simply getting started can seem utterly impossible as the blank screen (the computer, not the persona of the therapist) looms implacably in front of us. When I was a journalist reporting on live events, I lost count of the number of times I sat manic and miserable in front of my laptop computer, not having written a single word on the screen, with the deadline for my 1000-word article 30 minutes away and counting. Panic, gloom and an unshakeable conviction that a letter of dismissal and my P45 would be winging its way to me in the post the next day, probably took several years off my life. Yet, invariably, all it took in the end to get me up and running at full stretch was that first sentence or paragraph there in front of me in glorious black and white.

The point I am making is that trainees who are habitually fazed by essays before they have even started should not undervalue the process that takes place before the physical act of putting words on paper is carried out. Anthony Storr (1991: 273) takes up this theme

## On training to be a therapist

when he analyses those periods when writers and composers are unable to produce anything:

> Sometimes such spells of frustration occur in persons of manic-depressive temperament as a consequence of a mood-swing towards depression . . . In other instances the condition is a consequence of attempting to make a premature start upon a new piece of work, before sufficient time has been allowed for the process of incubation to take place . . . It is often very difficult for people with a powerful super-ego to feel that they are doing anything useful in the pre-liminary stages of a new piece of work, when day-dreaming, play-ing around with ideas, reading, listening, and passively hoping for the best, may all be part of bringing to birth the unformulated conception. As a result such people make false starts, and aim at premature perfection. It is important for them to appreciate the (admittedly one-sided) truth contained in the Chinese proverb 'There is nothing which cannot be achieved by non-action'.

Perhaps an even greater difficulty with embarking on a piece of written work concerns the 'post-parturition' process of deliver-ing one's creation to the world, where it will be scrutinized, judged, taken apart, and very possibly rejected. There is so much invested in an essay or case study in terms of what we give of ourselves, and concomit-antly our self-esteem, that it can almost seem better to keep the gesta-tion period going indefinitely. The labour pains that come with the birth of a written 'baby' that has been so painstakingly created and is then given away for assessment can feel excruciating.

Storr is also illuminating on this point. He talks about situ-ations where the person's identity has become so completely embodied in the work that its success or failure is entirely substituted for personal success or failure in interpersonal relations. In such cases, anxiety about being creatively blocked can reach such a pitch that the individual con-templates, and may attempt, suicide. Storr writes (1991: 273–4):

> When creative work has become as 'overdetermined' as this – that is, when it contains the whole of a person's self-esteem and sense of self – it becomes extremely difficult to pursue it. An element of play and an element of craftsmanship of a rather impersonal kind need to enter into all creative work. However important the work, it must also be fun to some extent; and work cannot be fun if every value in life is bound up with it . . . This projection upon the work of values which do not necessarily belong to it also prevents the achievement of 'psychical distance' from it . . .

# The dangers in playing it by the book

The concept of psychical distance seems especially relevant in terms of enabling students to free their minds from what can feel like overwhelming expectations, both from tutors and themselves. Perhaps the biggest misconception that can develop as a result of this pressure is a sense of having to pack everything and more into a piece of written work. So, what should be a relatively straightforward task becomes an impossible attempt to cover every possible angle on theory, include every quote that is even vaguely relevant, and put it all down on paper in a style that is a cross between Sigmund Freud and Charles Dickens.

Taking Storr's idea a little further, possibly the best way to master manic essay survival syndrome is to stand back from it and not only achieve a healthy distance from it, but also to view it afresh, focusing purely on what first came to mind when you thought of tackling that particular topic or case study. That might sound simple enough, but the difficulty is keeping it just that – simple. All too often the initial concept, which seemed relatively attractive and straightforward when it was conceived, becomes buried beneath a haze of overdetermined thinking.

In the end, it is too much thinking and not enough action that can be our worst enemy, a theme that is encapsulated in a comment made by Freud to Joan Riviere, which could be taken as a powerful antidote to essay anxiety. Freud's comment was referred to by Elliott Jaques in a fascinating paper dealing with creativity and middle age. Jaques writes (1965: 503, original emphasis):

> In her note 'A Character Trait of Freud's', Riviere (1958) describes Freud's exhorting her in connection with some psychoanalytic idea which had occurred to her. 'Write it, write it, put it down in black and white . . . get it out, produce it, make something of it – **outside you**, that is; give it an existence independently of you'.

Whether it is a case study, theoretical essay or any other category of written work, it can help to 'get it out' by thinking of the process as telling a story. Begin at the beginning, progress in narrative fashion through what you want to say about the topic or the client in question, and end with what seems to be a natural conclusion. That might sound too reductionist and simplistic, but it offers a basic framework for conceptualizing the task. It is then possible to build on this framework and elaborate by filling in the pieces gradually, like doing a jigsaw puzzle where the bigger picture is already in your mind and gradually takes shape as you insert each piece.

It is of course essential to fulfil the criteria demanded by those who will assess your work, and one should always be at pains to give the assessors exactly what they want in terms of the basic academic requirements, within the specific parameters laid down for that particular piece of work. Thus, if you are asked for a case study of up to 5000 words, do not be surprised if you submit 5500 words and have it thrown back at you regardless of the quality. If for example, you are specifically asked to talk about boundary issues and/or breaks and endings in the study, you can hardly complain if it is failed because you did not touch on those matters, even though you might have addressed just about every other clinical and theoretical issue it was possible to address.

What will ultimately make your essay successful, though, is getting down on paper in an accessible and orderly way what *you* regard as the salient features of the issue to be discussed and not what you think will impress intellectually or what someone else might expect of you. Underpinning your arguments with the use of pertinent quotes by authorities within the field is necessary and desirable, but what will influence the person marking your written work is your capacity for making *your* experience and understanding of the subject come to life.

In this respect, there is something of the true self versus false self scenario involved, and this pertains to far more than mere academic prowess; it goes to the very heart of our practice as therapists. In setting out to examine this concept, I have returned to the theme that began this chapter, namely the drawbacks in adhering too strictly to theory and excessive bookishness, looking at this thorny issue in the context of clinical practice, and the nature (and nurture) of our evolving selves as therapists.

A typical student's-eye view of the difficulty of correlating theory with practice is articulated by Natalie Gibb:

> *I feel the link between practice and theory is slightly fragmented, making it difficult to apply certain theories to certain clients, as I tend to keep the two parts of myself separate (i.e. emotive/intellect) and I have not discovered how I can combine them both. It is my belief that the theoretical formulations can only take us so far – 'By listening too readily to accepted theories and to what they lead the practitioner to expect, it is easy to become deaf to the unexpected' – Casement (1995).*

In considering how to integrate theory with practice, I believe what needs to be looked at above all are ways to avoid a stultifying, brittle kind of development through training that will leave our clients feeling unheard and uncared for because we are too preoccupied with trying to make them fit our precious theories rather than opening ourselves to the myriad of individual human responses and interaction.

## The dangers in playing it by the book

Furthermore, the adoption of a tunnel-visioned, one-dimensional view of therapy means we deny ourselves access to a wealth of methods and thought processes that could enrich our therapeutic armoury. The desirability of maintaining a fluid and open approach to dealing with clients' issues, one that that lends itself to genuine empathy, creativity and spontaneity, is being increasingly acknowledged, as witnessed by the spread of more integrative approaches and training courses. Yet, despite this more flexible and enlightened ethos permeating the therapy world, there are still many practitioners who rigidly uphold the need to maintain a particular method or approach at all costs.

I have myself come across more than one supervisor during training who has simply refused to contemplate any deviation from their designated methodology, and I know of several fellow trainees who had the same unnerving and often depressing experience. From the point of view of training, we are primarily in supervision to learn from someone with far greater experience, and for many people that is the best and most accessible way of learning. However, to attempt to work with someone who is by the nature of the relationship in a superior, judging capacity, and who will simply not allow the individuality and personal qualities of the supervisee to come into play, can be disagreeable, deskilling, and disheartening to a point where the trainee can seriously consider quitting, and may do so (see Chapter 5, where supervision is covered).

Furthermore, such arrogant, blinkered and defensive attitudes are bad practice both from a supervisory and a therapeutic point of view, something that has been underpinned time and again by telling evidence from close encounters of the therapeutic kind. Erwin Singer (1993: 366) sums this up nicely:

> *Above all, any worthwhile theory must include provisions for its own revision; otherwise, it is just a closed system, dogma, or pronouncement. The analyst offering interpretations on the basis of some preconceived theory about about presumed historical actualities, rather than on the basis of his direct comprehension and appreciation of the patient's psychological reality, to use Erikson's (1964) terms, is insulting.*

Ernesto Spinelli (1998: 90–2) covers the matter of differing theoretical approaches, and examines what works for clients and why in some detail. Spinelli cites amongst others, a review by Orlinsky and Howard (1986) of 1100 outcome studies, spanning 35 years, which shows that the one crucial factor in all cases of effective therapy is the bond that therapists form with their clients. The approach or orientation of

## On training to be a therapist

the therapist appears to be of little or no significance, nor do factors related to training or the nature or quality of the therapists' interpretations and interventions, something that has been consistently evidenced in similar studies. This would appear to deal a decisive blow to the one-dimensionalists, but in saying this we should be careful not to throw the baby out with the bath water.

I would not suggest for a moment that anyone who finds adhering closely to one approach is misguided or wrong. If it feels right for them to work within a framework that is fundamentally psychodynamic, person centred, transpersonal, or any of the bewildering array of therapies currently available, that is perfectly fine, as long as they do not shut out all possibility of deviation, innovation, spontaneity, or creativity should the therapeutic interaction demand it. This means responding to the client's needs in the context of his current situation, which is a uniquely individual and ever-changing scenario. It does not mean desperately trying to shoehorn the client into one's pet theory or theories come what may.

The desirability of having a single fundamental approach that underpins one's thinking and practice, whilst allowing for a more open or integrative way of being and doing, is, I believe, the ideal in terms of providing a platform from which to build oneself up as a better and more effective therapist. An approach with no solid foundation can easily become an *ad hoc* way of doing things that more or less involves making it up as you go along. This carries with it a danger of undisciplined thinking and resorting to quick fixes, which is potentially as inimical to our patients as over-rigidity.

Returning to the primacy of the therapeutic relationship itself, Spinelli (1998: 81–3) indicates that there is also research showing that paraprofessionals consistently achieve outcomes which are at least as good as, and often better than, those of professionals. I remember one of my tutors saying that the only real difference training makes is to enable us to think more clearly and responsibly about how and why we do what we do. In the light of all this, Spinelli (1998: 77–9) addresses what is regarded as therapeutic or transformational from the point of view of clients, who, after all, should be better placed than anyone to know.

Taking an overview of various studies, Spinelli identifies the warmth and friendliness of therapists, and their ability to accept, listen to, and talk to their clients as key factors in giving them a good experience of therapy. He offers a book entitled *On Being a Client* by David Howe (1993) as a seminal text for discovering what clients really want:

> *Summarizing many of these findings, Howe points out that, generally, clients tend to prefer therapists who seem to them to have*

## The dangers in playing it by the book

*their own personality, sense of humour and particular character-istic 'quirks'. Clients also typically tend to prefer engagement and dialogue with the therapists and tend to experience the therapist's unwillingness to engage verbally with them, or to remain silent, as being artificial, threatening, or rejecting . . .*

*Howe amplifies these findings by arguing that the therapeutic process itself is impaired when therapists fail to understand, or even attempt to understand, their clients. Worse, under such cir-cumstances, clients' sense of isolation is likely to increase when therapists seek to impose their own explanations on the client's experience . . .*

This would seem to indicate quite clearly that a therapist who rigidly espouses a particular theory or methodology rather than being himself or herself, is likely to be regarded as ineffective and pos-sibly even punitive or harmful by the client. As I am repeatedly at pains to stress, it is an indisputable fact that as trainees we are constrained to a large extent by the demands of tutors and supervisors. Yet, as we read, mark, learn and inwardly digest what is served up to us during training, our goal should be to take in from our teachers what we need to en-hance our own development, fighting at all costs to hold on tightly to our sense of self, or if you like our therapeutic essence. This ability to be our natural selves and to eschew acting in a certain way merely because we feel it is appropriate or expedient is what will make us more real and therefore more available to our clients in the therapeutic encounter.

Peter Lomas (1994: 11–12) puts it this way:

*These two facts about the nature of psychotherapy complement each other. If its aim is to reveal the patient's capacity to experi-ence life in a real way, then one can only expect this to happen if the therapist himself acts in the encounter as a real person: true experience has little chance of emerging in a false setting.*

My own inflexible approach undoubtedly lost me a client at a relatively early stage of my clinical work when I was still obsessed by the notion, based on my psychodynamic training, that a therapist must at all times maintain a 'blank screen' demeanour and not offer human responses.

The client, whom I will call Keith, was aged 38 and was suffering from depression brought on by the recent death of his mother at a relatively young age. The bereavement had triggered guilt as well as issues from the past. Keith always presented himself with a happy facade, in notable contrast to his anguished internal state, and more

**77**

than once he complained that I was not responsive to his cheery greetings. In what was to be our final session (he came to see me only six times) he opened by telling me that I seemed solemn and that I never asked him how he was and whether he had had a good week.

Keith then rang me to tell me he would be ending therapy and when I suggested we had one more session to discuss the matter he replied that he definitely wanted to end the sessions forthwith. He said: 'It's not that I don't like you, but because I find you so solemn and unresponsive I find it difficult to open up with you.'

Keith was absolutely right – I had been solemn and unresponsive. I was still adhering to what I thought was the 'correct' way to present oneself as a therapist and dismissing my natural inclination to offer spontaneous warmth. It would have been possible to analyse Keith's need for a cheery greeting in various ways, including his wish to extend the relationship beyond that of therapist–client, and to see it as his problem, as indeed my psychodynamic supervisor encouraged me to do. We did look at why Keith felt he wanted that type of response from me during our work together, but, significantly, I failed to see beyond what I convinced myself was a pathological need in him.

By not giving Keith the kind of empathic responses he so obviously needed at that time, I had failed to develop a therapeutic alliance with him. Thus he found it all too easy to walk away from someone whom he felt was not really listening to him, nor accepting him, and thus appeared not to be on his side. Now I look back, I have to ask what harm would have been done by returning his smile, and indulging, within reasonable limits, his small talk and his enquiries about my own welfare. Needless to say, I have not made that particular mistake again. I am not saying I always get it right by any means, but, as a result I feel much freer and more available in my encounters with clients. I am convinced that attending to the little things, the minutiae that can make human interaction so special, has made me a better therapist.

As Spinelli points out (1998: 91), clients regard the bond they form with their therapist as the key factor in effective therapy. They are prepared to indulge our foibles and fumblings provided they perceive us a genuine and empathic. Singer (1993: 366) is also useful on this point:

> *If the therapist has laboured honestly, it is most likely that the patient will forgive him an interpretive speculation which is incorrect. But the patient will not forgive the therapist's inability to perceive him correctly ... when the speculations are not rooted in the immediacy of experience arising from therapeutic encounters and collaborations, but are merely reflections of the doctor's*

# The dangers in playing it by the book

*sterile and schematized approach to the understanding of human development and human affairs, especially when this is coupled with his insistence that he must be right and his demand that the patient accept sooner or later some theoretical credo cherished by the therapist.*

I will offer two examples of therapists being real in an idiosyncratic but acceptable and ultimately therapeutic way. The first concerns a colleague of mine, who had been to see four therapists of varying approaches and personalities over a period of years. One of these was a woman who appeared on the surface to have very little in the way of clear-cut professional boundaries. She would offer my colleague cups of tea and coffee; dogs and children would occasionally run in and out of the consulting room, and there was, to a certain extent an ethos of 'anything goes'.

Despite this, my colleague said he found this woman by far the best therapist of the four because he felt she genuinely cared about him, listened to his issues, and offered a degree of warmth, empathy and understanding that the other therapists did not. Though she did not manifest what might be regarded by some as a suitably professional persona, nor did she offer generally accepted boundaries in the external sense, she clearly had sufficient internalized boundaries to offer herself as a containing and good enough therapist for my colleague's needs, and that in the final analysis was what counted.

The overall persona of this particular therapist could be summarized as demonstrably human, as opposed to being a therapeutic automaton, which is neither desirable nor therapeutic. As I said earlier, it is often the little things, the quirky individuality, and the willingness to deviate from the norm or take an acceptable risk that endears therapists to us and thereby strengthens the relationship.

This leads me to my second example of a therapist being real and 'non-textbook', in this case a comment made by my own therapist, a Jungian analyst, who I was seeing during my advanced training. I had come to therapy on this particular evening complaining that, for various reasons, I had not eaten for several hours, as witnessed by a series of audible tummy rumbles. I commented at the start of the session that I could hardly wait for the end of the session to come as I was looking forward to buying a portion of fish and chips from the local fish and chip shop, a delight I had not indulged in for some months. I then launched into the various issues that needed to be dealt with, almost forgetting about my hunger. When the 50 minutes was up, my therapist said: 'It's fish and chip time'. I congratulated her on coming up with such an appropriate and human ending to a session.

**79**

## On training to be a therapist

When theory and an over-arching need to do things 'correctly' begins to take precedence and starts getting in the way of genuine or congruent interaction, I suppose the question that needs to be asked is – why are we so scared of being ourselves? We *are* human after all, and as such we have idiosyncrasies and limits. Arguably, it is good to let our clients see these individual traits from time to time and to encourage them to accept a therapist who is not perfect but good enough. Whilst they look to us as 'experts', and even saviours, it can be said with some degree of certainty that people who come for help with psychological and emotional problems feel far more comfortable in the presence of someone who demonstrates ordinary humanity and fallibility, provided it does not actually impair the work (see Chapter 6), than a supremely clever but non-empathic, distant figure.

As a way of summarizing everything that has been discussed in this chapter, I believe it would be impossible to better the words of Carl Jung (1928: 361): 'Learn your theories as well as you can, but put them aside when you touch the miracle of the living soul. Not theories but your own creative individuality alone must decide.'

# 5   *Super*-vision syndrome and how to avoid it

The unconscious manifests itself in fascinating ways, which is why I found it especially intriguing when one of my colleagues on a training course habitually pronounced the word supervision as *super*-vision, with the accent firmly on the first two syllables. I noticed subsequently that my colleague was not alone in her unorthodox accentuation, there were other trainees who instinctively stressed the 'super', which led me to reach a telling conclusion about the supervisory relationship as a whole.

In the context of early supervisory experiences – and indeed many ongoing ones, too – this verbal parapraxis signalled a view of supervisors which, from the frequently infantilized standpoint of trainees, elevates those in supervisory roles to an almost deified status. Whether we are at the most basic level of training, or even, in some cases, when we are approaching therapeutic adulthood in the guise of professional registration, supervisors frequently seem to possess a kind of psychological radar that is from another stratosphere.

Though the syndrome of holding supervisors in awe may never totally go away, it is, of course, felt much more powerfully when we are in the earlier stages of training. In total contrast to our own inept fumblings and our struggle to work at the most simplistic level of human interaction, not a single nuance or unconscious mental manoeuvre appears to escape their superhuman understanding. The extraordinarily complex processes of the human mind have been the stuff of theory, counter-theory and ferocious intellectual jousting for generations, yet supervisors appear able to unlock their mysteries in the blink of an eye. I used to reckon my first external supervisor should wear a little blue and red Superman suit with an S for *Super*-visor on the front. I could only sit back in awe – and a degree of envy, too – as yet another brilliant insight was delivered with stunning ease.

As we fumble our way through presentations of case material in the sure and certain knowledge that whatever we say will be systematically inspected, dissected, and often tossed aside like last week's garbage, it is easy to feel dispirited and worthless by comparison as our supervisors home in like hawks swooping unerringly on their prey. And, as we sit there frozen to our chairs, what can often compound our discomfort is the feeling that we are not only subject to the inscrutable – perhaps that should be implacable – gaze of our omniscient supervisor, but also to the gleeful stare of our fellow supervisees looking on at the blood-letting like Madame Defarge at the guillotine.

If that seems like an exaggeration of the angst induced by the supervisory process, I would suggest that for many students this perception is more of a reality than a fantasy. Indeed, if difficulties and anxieties are not properly addressed as soon as possible, supervision can feel more like a process of deconstruction and attrition, as one trainee, Janet Higson, describes:

> *In supervision people can easily feel victimized or got at. Sometimes it is the approach of the supervisor that is the problem, but it is often because the trainee lacks confidence and the supervisor can be quite cruel, so it becomes a kind of persecutory thing. The crux of the problem is not being heard and not knowing where to go with the problem or anxiety.*

In attempting to put feelings of inferiority and worthlessness into context, the first thing to remember is that supervisors are operating with what might be termed a distinct tactical advantage, rather like a defending army being given the detailed attacking strategy of the invading force before they have even landed. Someone once said that hindsight is 20–20 and, whereas we as therapists are taking part in the session as it evolves with no knowledge of what will occur within those frequently tense and stressful 50 minutes, supervisors are working with the benefit of a retrospective viewpoint and are also free from the pressures and uncertainty of the session itself.

It is also important to acknowledge that every session can be seen in many different ways, and that one supervisor's analysis of the issues involved might, and frequently does, differ hugely from another's. Even if it were desirable, which is highly questionable, it would be virtually impossible to produce a definitive evaluation of any therapy session because each supervisor would view it through a subjective lens which is inevitably coloured by his or her own theoretical stance, personal approach and idiosyncrasies.

I remember how freeing it was to discover in my naïvety that my first ever supervisor was himself undergoing weekly supervision. Even though the idealization persisted to a degree, this colossus of therapeutic skill suddenly shrunk to almost human proportions in my eyes. So, I thought, with considerable glee, these demi-gods of therapy have feet of clay; they are neither omniscient nor infallible. They, too, must submit and justify themselves to a higher authority.

It is this ability to view supervisors in a 'real' light that is an important constituent of the learning process. In Kleinian terms, it involves moving from the standpoint of the paranoid-schizoid position to the depressive position. According to Hinshelwood (1991: 138), Klein postulated that the infant reached the depressive position when he or she became mature enough to integrate his or her fragmented perceptions of mother, bringing together the separately good and bad versions. For trainees this means moving from a view of one's supervisor as all good (or in some cases, all bad) to seeing them as possessing both positive and negative attributes at the same time.

I have been fortunate to have had a series of wonderful supervisors who have given me a priceless therapeutic schooling. However, whilst they were insightful and technically astute in their different ways, each one had their foibles, and, dare I say it, blind spots. These 'faults' did not in any way seriously negate their insights and their ability to pass on their clinical expertise, but it was necessary to be aware of their particular idiosyncracies in order to bracket them and thus allow a more rounded consideration of the issues at hand.

If all this sounds somewhat negative, it must be stated here and now that supervision is arguably the most valuable component of any training course. In observing how experienced practitioners operate and being able to benefit from their feedback, we are offered an opportunity to learn by a kind of osmosis from someone who has 'been there, seen it and done it', which in any line of work, or human endeavour, is an invaluable route for self-development. In other words, the fact that a supervisor has encountered, worked with and thought through a myriad of therapeutic situations that we, as trainees, have possibly not even contemplated, can greatly help to enrich our thinking and practice and move us on to new levels of competence.

Responses to student questionnaires underpinned this line of thinking. Supervision emerged time and again as the major source of learning, support and inspiration for trainees. Here are just three examples:

## On training to be a therapist

*Ewan Gillon: Supervision is the ace card in training . . . You can learn a lot from supervision and it can be very self-affirming – which I believe is one of its functions. It is also very important in allowing supervisors to keep a check on what the trainees are doing.*

*Amanda Croucher: It is very helpful – essential – to have the supervisor's (and other supervisees') input into the details of what is happening with the client, the unconscious communications you haven't picked up, and also to feel that 'the buck doesn't stop' with you.*

*Riann Croft: Supervision saved my life really. I had a horrendous time on my training course . . . and I considered leaving, but my external supervisor clearly valued me and valued my work, and his nurturing allowed me to internalize that my work was of high quality even though the message from my course tutors was negative.*

Despite these, and many other positive affirmations of supervision, getting the most from the supervisory process is, in the majority of cases, not simply a matter of sitting back and letting it happen. In order to obtain what we as trainees need for our development, there has to be a conscious effort on our part to maximize the supervisory interaction so that supervisor and supervisee are working together in a way that affords mutual respect and understanding and allows for, indeed actively encourages, nurturing and growth of the person receiving the supervision.

I place considerable emphasis on the words 'conscious effort' because when trainees complain that they are not getting much from supervision or finding it unhelpful, and sometimes even traumatic and deconstructive, they have often allowed themselves to become passive 'bit part' players in a scenario that by its very nature and ideals should be one of joint endeavour. It is therefore incumbent on us as trainees to make it clear to supervisors what we require to facilitate our growth as practitioners, and what we need to feel valued and comfortable within the context of the supervisory hour (or however long the session may be).

In an interview for this book, Diane Rees-Roberts, a supervisor and tutor at Westminster Pastoral Foundation, offered some helpful thoughts on how supervision can seem from a trainee's point of view and how it might ideally be perceived:

*It takes a long time to know how to use supervision. The whole process can be scary when you start because you are not sure what*

## *Super*-vision syndrome and how to avoid it

*the expectations are. The relationship with the supervisor is very important, and should primarily enable you to learn from the supervisor. If you feel the supervisor is critical it can be difficult and inhibits presentation of case material. The best supervision is when you feel free to say whatever you feel and think, however outrageous.*

This is fine in principle and should certainly be encouraged, but given that the reality of the situation is that supervisors are not only vastly more experienced, but in many cases sitting in judgement on us during training, it can seem impossible for us to make ourselves heard and to attempt to get our needs met, especially if that involves making waves by challenging or disagreeing with the supervisor's way of doing things. Fear of failure and poor evaluation is discussed by Zaro, Barach, Nedelman and Dreiblatt (1978: 9) in the context of a scenario that can leave the trainee feeling caught in an impossible situation:

*In our supervision of students we find that at times they interpret the demands on them as a 'double bind' situation; that is, they are asked to be open and honest about their difficulties, but are simultaneously evaluated by supervisors on the number and extent of these difficulties. Conflicts such as these need to be worked out in individual supervisory and evaluative relationships; however, they illustrate the complicated nature of the psychotherapy teaching process.*

The harsh truth is that often there is a power differential which, sadly, can be exploited by supervisors who, for whatever reason, enjoy using their position to infantilize or undermine trainees and thereby reinforce their own sense of importance. This was emphasized by the comments of student Janet Higson above, who talked of the potential for cruelty and persecution on the part of supervisors, and it is reinforced in a very concrete way by another student, Elizabeth Moran, who suggests that 'Safeguards should be in place to ensure supervisors are constructively critical but not persecutory'.

I must stress that in my experience supervisors of the latter kind are in the minority, but they do exist and, in contrast to the wholly nurturing experiences of the trainees described above, many students find the process both deskilling and emotionally disturbing. Having said earlier that I found my own supervisors for the most part nurturing and helpful, I must also say that I have more than once found myself in a position where I needed to struggle desperately not just to be heard and validated but also to retain a sense of self, and to hold on to what I

## On training to be a therapist

believed was the most effective way for me personally to function as a therapist.

What I, and some of my fellow students, found especially difficult was to retain one's individuality and thought processes in the face of intense pressure to go along with the supervisor's approach as the only way. Being with a supervisor who adopts and insists on a rigid, dogmatic or blinkered approach that does not allow for any sort of lateral thinking or individual creativity can be a nightmare for trainees at any stage of their clinical development. This can be stifling and demoralizing for the supervisee, and can be inimical to the therapeutic process between supervisee and client, as highlighted in Chapter 4.

Sussman (1992: 254) offers some interesting thoughts on the topic of supervisor grandiosity. He suggests that supervisors can nurture students by helping them deal with what he terms 'narcissistic deflation' as a result of dealing with difficult or hostile patients. He also says that supervisors can assist trainees in mourning the loss of their idealized personal aspirations. He then offers a caveat:

> As Brightman (1984–1985) argues, such a process can be disrupted when supervisors have not come to terms with their own grandiosity, and present themselves as all-knowing or lacking in the capacity for uncertainty. Indeed, the unconscious agenda of the supervisor is an important topic in its own right, and one that has been largely neglected. Langs (1979) notes the dearth of literature on the supervisor's countertransferences and expressions of psychopathology within the supervisory process. Teitlebaum (1990) also points to the reluctance on the part of many supervisors to look beyond the therapist's learning problems, and to consider their own teaching problems and the emotional sources from which they spring.

The theme of being stunted by a supervisor's personal approach, brings up another associated difficulty for trainees, namely being 'caught in a crossfire' of differing approaches. I have also found myself in this situation, having to contend with supervisors who were almost diametrically opposed in their thinking and practice. This occurred during an early part of my training when my internal supervisor was strictly psychodynamic and my external supervisor at my placement favoured a far more integrative way of working with a highly cognitive element.

At first I felt I was being pulled so vigorously in opposite directions that I was almost torn apart. As a new boy to the whole business of therapy I felt compelled to please both supervisors, which, of course, was an impossibility and left me feeling worthless and extremely unhappy. It was only through my own personal therapy that I came to realize that if I was to extricate myself from this situation and get what I needed out of it, I had to be assertive and make my feelings known to both supervisors.

As it happened, they both responded positively, acknowledging my difficulties and offering a more 'accepting' way of working with me. This did not lessen or weaken their personal credos but offered more flexibility and room for discussion. Having been utterly stifled, I felt I could at least breathe again, and begin to assimilate what I saw as the positive aspects of their thinking and practice, and move forward. These situations are not always so clear-cut and easy to resolve by any means, but failure to at least attempt to be heard and have one's individuality accepted and respected will inevitably lead to frustration and hinder the learning process. If all else fails and the supervisor is not prepared to compromise, it is, in my opinion, far better to leave and seek another placement than to suffer in silence and risk becoming therapeutically stuck, resentful and depressed.

Some may ask why, if I was undergoing a psychodynamic training, I took up a placement with someone who did not espouse that way of working in its purest sense. The fact is, as many students will testify, that in these days when the number of students in training is increasing all the time, it is difficult and sometimes seemingly impossible to obtain any placement at all and occasionally one has to take whatever is on offer. As a result, trainees can feel grateful and beholden to the placement to a point where not towing the line or daring to question a supervisor's pronouncements even in a minor way can seem risky or wrong.

One of the most common misconceptions or traps arising from supervision is the feeling that we have to rush out and incorporate every single suggestion our supervisors make in the very next session with our client. Thus, for example, if your supervisor tells you that there appear to be unresolved Oedipal issues with a particular patient, it is only too easy to go into the session with the word 'Oedipal' buzzing round your brain like a demented wasp. Regardless of the content of the session you are determined to deliver the sting at the first possible opportunity and, seizing on the flimsiest excuse, you make an interpretation about the child–parent triangle that is as inappropriate as it is crass.

Even if the suggestion from your supervisor seems in line with your own thinking and methodology it is arguably the best policy in most cases to adopt a 'wait and see' policy, bearing the thought or insight in mind and using it as a base for achieving further insight or understanding rather than offering it up on a platter like reconstituted food. There may, of course, be a legitimate reason to use the supervisor's

## On training to be a therapist

suggestion in the precise form he or she presented it, especially when we have been stuck on a particular issue with a client. In such cases a good supervisory analysis or interpretation can help us unstick the situation and move the client on. Leaving aside the learning process, that is precisely what the process of supervision is about: facilitating us as supervisees to facilitate the client in changing his situation or making sense of a problem that seemed unresolvable.

Having a good supervisor whom we admire and respect can hold an inherent danger as well as a positive side. A tendency to idealize can develop whereby we accept everything the supervisor says and does without questioning it or analysing what it means in terms of our own thinking. This in turn can lead us to model ourselves on the supervisor to such an extent that our own therapeutic persona becomes repressed or even obliterated. There is absolutely nothing wrong with modelling oneself on a competent practitioner for whom we have a healthy regard provided we keep any veneration and deference in perspective and retain a sense of who we are and how we feel the client is best served and treated.

Patrick Casement, who is a perennial source of inspiration on the subject of supervision, points to the danger of placing too much reliance on supervisors' dicta per se. Having stressed that trainee therapists need to be professionally held by a supervisor who believes in their capabilities, Casement writes (1995: 23–4, original emphasis):

> However, students need to be able to develop a style of working which is compatible with their own personality; so there will be something essential missing if he or she becomes too much of a **pastiche** of the training analyst, or the supervisor, however unconscious that may be. Amongst the pitfalls of a supervisor (and here I draw upon what I have learned from those I have supervised) is the danger of offering too strong a model of how to treat the patient. This can mislead students into learning by a false process, borrowing too directly from a supervisor's way of working rather than developing their own. Some students can be seriously undermined in this way, feeling as if the treatment (or even the patient) has been taken over by the supervisor.

Many writers and theoreticians advocate the drawing up of a contract between supervisor and supervisee in much the same way that a therapist negotiates a contract with a client. As well as the inclusion of such basic matters as the time and place of the meeting, the frequency of sessions and related matters of detail, the issue of boundaries within the supervisory relationship also seems to be an important contractual item, as is confidentiality. However, in terms of enabling

**88**

## *Super*-vision syndrome and how to avoid it

trainees to obtain maximum benefit from supervision, it is my belief that these fundamentals, whilst essential for a good working relationship, are very much subsidiary to the need to focus on the supervisory relationship itself, that is to say the interaction, expectations, and the facilitation of learning and clinical expertise that a trainee might reasonably expect from a good supervisor.

Steve Page and Val Wosket (1995: 65) suggest that the supervisory relationship can be thought of as having two different aspects, (1) the affective or qualitative relationship between the supervisor and supervisee, and (2) the working or functional relationship. They suggest that the supervisory relationship functions best when it contains the basic principles of all good human relationships:

> *A supervision relationship which offers the Rogerian core conditions of respect, empathy and congruence (Rogers 1961) can, we firmly believe, enormously enhance the quality of the supervision work. The establishment of such a relationship builds a safe and secure framework within which the supervisee can risk exploring difficult and even painful issues which, if worked through, can prove extremely efficacious to the counsellor's client work. Though hierarchical, the supervision relationship can be experienced as facilitative and even therapeutic . . . 'It is not threatening in that the student knows I am not judging. I am trying to help by providing essentially the same relationship the student should be providing in therapy'.*
>
> *(Freeman 1992: 221)*

The problem we are faced with as trainees is that the gulf between these supervisory ideals and actually obtaining them in practice can seem huge. The circumstances of our supervision by their very nature imbue the relationship with overtones of power, judgement and intellectual superiority or rivalry. Also, the relationship is subject to the same constraints, vicissitudes, and issues of trust and understanding as any other relationship. The question of parental, superego or transferential issues can be another important factor and this is addressed by Sandra Thomas (1997: 65):

> *How successful the trainee has become in resolving conflicts with parental figures will determine which attributes will be actualized during supervision, such as uncritical acceptance, hostile opposition, or intellectual surrender. The resolution of such conflicts indicates that several developmental lines have to be crossed first. An important prerequisite to learning is the establishment of a learning*

*alliance that is based on a mutuality of goals and is dependent on how the trainee and supervisor can relate to each other.*
*(Szecsody 1990)*

Thomas's references to crossing developmental lines might suggest that there should be an interplay or overlap between supervision and therapy. The two should not be treated as conjoint and interchangeable because the processes could become blurred and diluted. However, from a trainee's point of view, some facilitation and recognition of the supervisee's personal difficulties and blocks may be beneficial inasmuch as they affect not only the work with the client but also the trainee's professional development generally. Being in supervision with a supervisor who is sensitive to a trainee's personal areas of difficulty and offers empathy and support is truly a blessing. However, supervision is not a place to resolve one's emotional and personal difficulties; that is the domain of personal therapy. Establishing a good balance and appropriate boundaries between the two can provide a valuable superstructure of nurturing and support during a phase of much uncertainty and regression.

In this context, we can return to Winnicott's notions of play leading to creativity and a search for the self (1999: 54). This was mentioned in the Introduction when talking about the need for students to find enjoyment and even fun in training instead of simply pursuing that all-important piece of paper at the end with a grim determination that does not allow for any satisfaction from the process itself. So with supervision, Winnicott's idea of psychotherapy taking place in the overlap of two areas of playing, that of therapist and client, can be transposed to supervision taking place in the overlap of playing between supervisor and supervisee.

Winnicott's notion of 'potential space' would also be relevant. In looking at play as facilitating the baby's move away from its mother, Winnicott says that the playground is the potential space between the mother and baby or joining the mother and baby (1999: 47). In the case of supervision, the potential space would be the supervisory process itself in which the trainee learns how to be creative and 'real' as part of his or her move towards maturation as a therapist.

It must be stressed again that the whole area of the supervisory relationship is fraught with potential difficulties in as much as one is talking about the attempted collaboration of two people with an inherent power differential, often from wildly contrasting backgrounds, and sometimes with mismatched objectives and ideals. A process of acceptance and negotiation is essential on both sides, and this can entail risk-taking and courage on the part of the trainee. The concept of socio-cultural issues of difference is taken up by Mary Spencer (2000: 518) in

## *Super*-vision syndrome and how to avoid it

a statement that could serve as a more general template for what can be achieved in supervision given a genuine meeting of minds:

> *Such differences may lead to difficulty if avoided or unacknowledged, so that we are not really making contact, not meeting the other in supervision. This leads to a distancing gap, a growing separateness and false or proxy-self communication. Alternatively, if a potential space opens up in the supervisory triangle of relationship – a space for thinking and working creatively together so that issues of difference can be addressed constructively – then, paradoxically, we are really meeting the other in the encounter and making more direct communication. The results can be enabling and enriching for the supervisor, the counsellor and the client.*

When talking of the need to be open and honest with one another, the issue of countertransference raises its often unprepossessing head. Feelings arising in the supervisor or supervisee in response to the other, whether on a personal or professional level, can be not only an impediment to the work, but also inimical to the client if not owned and addressed. In some cases it may be difficult and even impossible to reveal such feelings, for example if you were to find yourself attracted to your supervisor. This is something I have not only experienced myself but have also come across in other trainees, in one instance to an extent where the unspoken and therefore unrequited passion of the trainee became virtually the sole motivation and meaning for attending the supervision session.

In such cases, when it seems impossible to bring difficult or embarrassing feelings into the open, it is arguably enough to be fully aware of them and the effect they are having on the work, and to attempt to bracket them and view the interaction as a purely professional one. In this context, one's personal therapy would be the right and proper place to take those feelings in order to work through them and make them more manageable. In the case of what might be termed ordinary, everyday feelings, such as envy, inferiority, or irritation, the only real way forward is to disclose them, which for a trainee can be equally difficult without the explicit encouragement of the supervisor.

I remember one of my early supervisors, who was some 10 years younger than I was, taking me aside and asking me if I felt resentful at being supervised by a younger man. This irritated me because it was something I was certainly not aware of on a conscious level. I told him of my irritation and, taking a deep breath and praying that my insolence would not result in a metaphorical black mark for my course assessment, I asked him to consider why he had brought the subject up

## On training to be a therapist

and what meaning it had for him. On reflection, it transpired that he felt not only guilt but a degree of concern or even pity for me at my having to suffer such a perceived indignity and had therefore been treating me as if I were somehow fragile. We talked it through and ended up laughing about it. I felt considerably more respect for him because of his willingness to be open. Would that these interactions were always so simple and enriching.

Page and Wosket (1995: 103) identify two types of supervisory countertransference, syntonic and illusory. They define syntonic countertransference as: 'The response of the supervisor (or counsellor) to the transference material being directed towards them by the supervisee (or client).' They give an example of a supervisee who perceives the supervisor as a caring, parental figure. The supervisor can have two types of response to this transferential material, either to feel nurturing and protective towards him (a 'concordant' response), or to tell him to stand on his own two feet (a 'complementary' response). Both responses are syntonic countertransference insofar as they are a direct response to the supervisee's transference.

Illusory countertransference is explained as: 'The unconscious psychological material of the supervisor directed at the supervisee.' This might, for example, be feelings of resentment at having to nurture the supervisee because she already gives so much emotionally to her own clients, a response born out of her own neediness. Page and Wosket conclude by saying that it is imperative for the supervisor to contain such responses in supervision and take them to their own therapy.

Clearly all feelings raised by the presence and persona of the other in the supervisory relationship need ideally to be examined in some form in order to remove any blocks to the work. Like all of these supervisory issues, though, the onus on the trainee to have, as the politicians say, a full and frank discussion, with someone who is perceived as being more experienced, more insightful, and more powerful, can be overwhelming and therefore very little or nothing gets said. However, in terms of securing for oneself – and for our clients – the most enlightening and helpful supervision, it can be argued that discretion should rarely be seen as the better part of valour.

It is also important to be aware that our fellow supervisees can have a negative or repressive effect on us and our development. Given the competitive and judgemental elements of any training course, the issue of sibling rivalry is almost bound to be felt in the arena of supervision where the supervisor can be perceived as not merely having a good deal of influence on the assessment process but also to be favouring one student at the expense of another. This can be compounded by the fact that some supervisees not only find it easier to present material in front of others, but also appear keen to score points from fellow supervisees and thus win the favour of the supervisor. The fact that this may be 'all in the mind' does not matter; the point is that supervisees need to know they are valued, listened to and treated equally compared to their peers and, if the supervisor is not able or willing to make that happen, then it is up to us as trainees to make ourselves heard however difficult that might be.

The supervisor mentioned earlier, with whom I had a constructive interaction over the issue of age difference, spoke to me in confidence on another occasion and asked me if I found it difficult to claim space for myself in the sessions. He said that he perceived I was somewhat reticent in our discussions and analysis of case material compared to my fellow supervisee. On reflection I said that whilst I was not meaning to criticize the other supervisee, I did feel she was difficult to interrupt when she was in full flow, giving vent to her opinions and interpretations at some length, which was quite often. My supervisor told me quite simply to make a conscious effort to make my thoughts and insights heard and to claim the space that I was entitled to, which, though not easy initially, proved to be very freeing and helpful to my development once I gained the confidence to do so.

In a highly instructive paper on supervising pairs, which could arguably be applied just as appropriately to groups of three or four supervisees, Michael Jacobs (1994) draws attention to the issue of peer competition when he talks of the supervisor's need to ensure that the non-presenter is interactive and does not become an observer or sleeping partner:

> *It is tempting for supervisees to imagine that the only wisdom comes from the supervisor – or to neglect the insights of the colleague because of competitive feelings, which make it seem as if the other is 'scoring a point'. (Rivalry and competition is clearly one of the issues that can be present in a threesome – any one of the three may feel it. Feeling excluded is a concomitant reaction to this.)*

Jacobs adds another important point, which follows on from this, when he says that the non-presenter can afford to free associate totally and is much more at liberty to do this than the supervisor who has to combine free-floating attention (i.e. being open to whatever comes up) with keeping the ground rules, and the work going, as well as facilitating the supervisory relationships:

> *The non-presenter therefore has a potentially unique position in their freedom, and should be encouraged therefore not just to be a*

**93**

## On training to be a therapist

*supervisor who makes typical supervisor's interventions, but if experiencing other feelings, to say so; even to be a 'maverick' – e.g. the non-presenter might say, 'I am experiencing not wanting to get at all engaged in this discussion' – which is more difficult for the supervisor to say – yet the non-presenter's remark may be precisely what is needed to make a breakthrough with a difficult client.*

These factors underline the fact that supervisees can come to realize and to believe that they can contribute as much – and on occasions maybe more – to a session as their fellow supervisees and their supervisors, too. In the context of self-belief, I recall having particular difficulty with one external supervisor who refused to contemplate allowing me to work in a way that deviated even remotely from her rigid approach. When I mentioned to my internal college supervisor – who was invariably nurturing and supportive – that this was destroying my confidence and making me thoroughly confused, she asked me to consider the following question: Did I believe, she asked, that if I followed my instincts and used my own natural approach, I could be as effective as my external supervisor would be if she were seeing my clients. After due consideration, I said that I believed I could, and my internal supervisor said she concurred with my view.

I say this not to trumpet my own abilities but to illustrate how trainees can easily fall prey to *super*-vision syndrome, not merely because we elevate supervisors to superhuman levels but also because we can become ensnared in a crippling spiral of self-doubt that vitiates our belief in our own experience, individuality and ability. Dave Mearns (2000: 127) offers a heartening perspective on this issue:

> *As a supervisor, one of the most important things for me to remember is that my supervisee is a different person from me; it is not my job to constrain my supervisee to model his work on myself. There may be aspects of my working which he chooses to adopt, but in most areas he will have his own style, and in some instances his functioning will be superior to mine. I think it is most important for a supervisor and supervisee to discuss issues like this as an aspect of their work together.*

There will doubtless be many trainees wishing all supervisors were as allowing and affirming as this. Yet, in Mearns's last sentence we find confirmation that achieving the best from supervision from a trainee's perspective necessitates a joint effort incorporating mutual respect and honesty. This is amplified in an empathic and sensitive

## *Super*-vision syndrome and how to avoid it

way by Freddie Strasser (1999: 119) looking back on his wide-ranging supervisory experiences with trainees and experienced therapists:

> *This experience taught me that the term 'supervision' in itself might impede successful training because it can increase the possible feeling of defensiveness of the supervisees. Supervisees inevitably try to present their cases with what in their perception is 'good therapy'. When they feel criticised, emotion surges and a resistance to listening develops. Sometimes supervisors cannot resist having an attitude of superiority. This is evidently counterproductive, even if merely manifested in a paternalistic manner . . .*
>
> *In order to alleviate these situations, I always discuss with groups or individuals the process between us. I also encourage them to present their problems and failures, disclosing their vulnerabilities as well as their successes. I consider it a strength and not a weakness if we are able to become aware of our emotions and overcome the desire to protect our self-esteem. My role in supervision is mainly to listen, empathically prompt and explain my way of working and the assumptions behind it.*

I have not attempted in this chapter to provide an exhaustive examination of all aspects of supervision, focusing instead on those issues that may help trainees get the most out of their supervisory encounters. Supervision is a vast and vitally important area of the therapeutic process, as witnessed by the huge amount of literature on the subject, but too often the feelings, needs and concerns of supervisees, especially those in training, are not addressed in a way that is as comprehensive, open and helpful as it could be.

Students do have the power to be heard and validated, and thus enhance their ability to offer their clients therapy that is valuable and real. This will not be the case if we persist in seeing supervisors as superior beings from another therapeutic planet. To a greater or lesser degree, the supervisory process can be whatever we want to make of it. And when *super*-vision syndrome starts to blind and inhibit us, always remember – hindsight makes geniuses of us all.

# 6    Caution: go-slow
area ahead

Those of us long enough in the tooth to remember will recall that the
actor, Herbert Lom, had an altogether different screen persona before he
became immutably typecast as the demented boss of Peter Sellers, a.k.a.
Inspector Clouseau, in the hilariously madcap Pink Panther films. For
some reason best known to those in central casting, the urbane Lom, of
the furrowed brow and lilting mid-European accent, was picked out to
star in a 1960s television series called *The Human Jungle* as an all-seeing,
all-knowing psychiatrist, the absolute antithesis of his brilliantly manic
Pink Panther policeman characterization.

In those wonderfully naïve but compelling old dramas,
Lom's omniscient psychiatrist would spend what seemed like just a few
short hours with a patient suffering from some dreadful mental afflic-
tion. Then, suddenly, just when all hope of recovery appeared lost, he
would come up with some utterly brilliant interpretation or insight which
spirited away the depression, mental block, amnesia, or whatever it was
that had immobilized the patient, and restored the grateful individual to
psychic wholeness in what equated to no more than a nanosecond in
real-life psychotherapeutic terms.

Would that it were so simple? Not so fast. The dream of
instant nirvana in the consulting room is totally understandable from
the point of view of our clients, who in 99 per cent of cases would
understandably opt for a Lom-style deliverance, both from the point of
view of finance and the avoidance of prolonged psychic pain. However,

## Caution: go-slow area ahead

the first thought that occurs is one of naked self-interest, namely if therapy were that straightforward and instantaneous most of us would be out of work fairly swiftly!

On a more serious note, the notion of instant solutions to problems is still very much an underlying psychotherapeutic fantasy and one that can bedevil trainees. Having said that, I am sure there are times when even the most highly qualified and experienced practitioner would also give their right arm to come up with a life-changing formula which not only gets them out of a seemingly impenetrable situation but also makes them look good in the eyes of the client.

The desire for therapeutic second-sight is based to a large extent on the belief that it is not okay to remain in a state of unknowing, even for a temporary period, a feeling that is by no means confined to therapy. This insidious syndrome has its roots in our increasingly science-based world where it has become de rigueur to seek nothing less than watertight answers and explanations for every situation, phenomenon and question, whether it be scientific, philosophical, spiritual, practical, or whatever. Stephen Hawking's brilliant television series on the origins of the universe ('Stephen Hawking's Universe', 1997), for which the rationale was a quest to find 'a theory of everything', was a prime example of this kind of scientific tunnel vision.

This obsession with results and evidence is highlighted by Ernesto Spinelli (2001: 3), Academic Dean of Regent's College, School of Psychotherapy and Counselling, who refers to a statement by Otto Kernberg, President of the International Psychoanalytic Association, in which Kernberg identifies a tendency for training institutes to infantilize psychoanalytic trainees and also highlights 'a lack of concern for their total educational experience'. Spinelli says Kernberg's statement could apply to all brands of psychotherapy training, not just psychoanalytic. He writes:

> *Psychotherapy enters the new millennium aware of Kernberg's (and many others) concerns and seeks to address these by speaking a new form of psychobabble – technobabble. It is obsessed with 'evidence of this' and 'proof of that'. It wants those who practice psychotherapy to perceive themselves as being 'mechanics of the mind' who will get their clients into better shape, all revved up and raring to go . . . All well and good. But . . . As yet, that element of the 'mysterious' that infuses all forms of psychotherapy remains ineffable, unyielding to the prodding of 'evidence-based analyses' and the like . . . So . . . our response to Kernberg's concerns regarding infantilisation of trainees is not that of a shift toward more adult relations but, rather, that of speaking in terms*

## On training to be a therapist

*of 'service providers' and 'customers' whose relations are deline-
ated and contained by formal agreements that provide an empty
kind of quality – the kind that cannot mention the existence of the
mysterious.*

From the standpoint of trainees there is a natural and understandable reluctance or fear of staying with a process of un-knowing.
Unlike medicine where procedures for restoring health are mostly far
more concrete and clearly defined, therapy is a journey into what can be
a black hole of uncertainty where even the most accomplished practitioner has no formulaic or ready made answers to call on. Working with
a client who does not appear to be moving or changing in any way, and
thus making the therapy seem totally stuck, can leave a trainee feeling
deskilled and useless, especially in the early stages of training.

The natural response is desperately to search one's mind
and come up with a life-changing interpretation or a practical piece of
advice that lifts the patient Lom-style out of his therapeutic impasse in a
trice, or face the prospect of losing the plot, one's credibility (such as it
is!) and the client. There is, however, much more to be lost through
offering quick fixes, and plenty to be gained by tolerating the uncertainty and containing it. What we can gradually come to understand and
to experience in practice is that during this time of apparent 'being and
nothingness', to appropriate Jean-Paul Sartre's eponymous book title,
there are very often thought processes and insights being conceived and
evolving. They will be allowed into consciousness, where they can be
acted on, when the client, having been appropriately held and contained
by the therapist, feels ready to make use of them.

It is necessary to state, however, that there is a practical
reality to the angst that accompanies feelings of therapeutic impotence
because as trainees we do have to prove our competence to tutors,
supervisors – and, of course, ourselves. The feeling that we have to
present a client whose graph of psychic health shows a sustained, even
dramatic, upward curve can therefore be quite overwhelming. Furthermore, we need ongoing patients in order to notch up the number of
hours required for our training, and any fears about losing clients can be
exacerbated by feelings of clinical ineffectiveness.

In attempting to dispel this self-imposed directive to work
extra hard and come up with Freud- or Klein-like deductions of pure
genius, it is useful to think of therapy as taking place in different phases
in which the client gradually builds up trust within a carefully deline-
ated framework. When therapy appears stuck the client may not yet be
ready to move to the next level and allow you access to the more deeply
hidden regions of his or her inner world. If we attempt to force clients to

# Caution: go-slow area ahead

lower their carefully assembled defences, the consequences can be disastrous, possibly leading to the termination of therapy.

The other great temptation, that of offering a 'sticking plaster', reassurance, or even blandishments, to make the pain or anxiety go away, usually has the same effect, or rather non-effect, as when a friend says 'Don't worry, it'll all work out for the best', thus completely denying the person's feelings and making them feel unheard. This must be qualified to a certain extent, however, because there can be times when people suffering mental turmoil do not want to be too deeply understood. Carl Jung (1973: 10) offers a helpful insight:

> For the purposes of therapy . . . it is highly important for the analyst to admit his lack of understanding from time to time, for nothing is more unbearable for the patient than to be always understood. The latter in any case relies too much upon the mysterious insight of the doctor, and, by appealing to his professional vanity, lays a dangerous trap for him. By taking refuge in the doctor's self-confidence and 'profound' understanding, the patient loses all sense of reality, falls into a stubborn transference, and retards the cure.

There are times when we can attempt to move things on, if the therapeutic alliance is strong enough. However, in order to progress in any meaningful way we can, in most cases, only move at the speed the client dictates. If that means snail's pace, so be it. I was seeing a client during the latter stages of my training who appeared to be offering me a full and frank picture of her internal world fairly early on in the therapy, and went through obvious hell to do so. There then followed several months of what felt like exceptionally laborious 'progress' – two steps forward, then one and a half backwards, and occasionally going round in ever-decreasing circles. I managed with some difficulty to stay with her and, with the help of my supervisor, to resist all temptation to try to offer some kind of magical solution in an attempt to move things on.

As I carried out what I saw as ineffectual 'maintenance' work week after week, I often wondered why she bothered to come to see me. Then, lo and behold, after she had been coming for about 18 months, she suddenly came out with a series of 'heavy' disclosures about her childhood, expressing feelings of shame and anger about the abuse she had been subjected to as a child that she would surely not have revealed if I had tried to force the pace. Indeed, had I attempted to do so, I am convinced she would have felt stripped of her defences and might even have left therapy.

## On training to be a therapist

Winnicott (1999: 117) highlights the importance of following the patient's lead:

*This glimpse of the baby's and child's seeing the self in the mother's face, and afterwards in a mirror, gives a way of looking at analysis and at the psychotherapeutic task. Psychotherapy is not making clever and apt interpretations; by and large it is a long-term giving the patient back what the patient brings. It is a complex derivative of the face that reflects what there is to be seen. I like to think of my work this way, and to think that if I do this well enough the patient will find his or her own self, and will be able to exist and to feel real.*

What the client brings may be their own feeling of being stuck or unable to effect changes in their life, which can get projected into the therapist and can prompt the therapist to act out by trying to 'unstick' the situation. In such a case it seems appropriate to interpret to the client that perhaps they feel stuck and would like you to effect a miracle cure. And, although some will not go along with this, I believe it is also useful to state explicitly that therapy is about working through the anxiety and the difficult feelings, not working magic.

I remember complaining to my own therapist, whom I experienced as being highly effective overall, that after some 12 months of therapy I had not made significant progress with one particular area of difficulty. She replied that the process of therapy can be likened to the work of a sculptor who begins a sculpture by working on a formless hunk of stone. Every tiny chip he makes changes the shape of the block, however imperceptibly, she said. That image made an indelible impression on me, and, I have to confess, I have 'plagiarized' it and used it with more than one of my own clients!

One of the most important things trainees can do in order to dispel feelings of impotence in slow-moving therapeutic encounters is to realize and accept not just their own limitations, but the limitations of therapy itself. I am not suggesting that therapy does not work nor that it cannot change and improve people's lives; quite the opposite, as I indicated in Chapter 3 when responding to the charges of the anti-therapy brigade. However, I believe the first thing trainees should do is to rid themselves of any notion of cure in the medical sense.

If you asked clients what they were seeking in therapy it is a fair bet that they would come up with things like 'to feel whole, together, happy, not bothered by feelings of inferiority and guilt or weighed down by depression, able to function fully and to feel fulfilled on a day to day basis'. Fair enough, you might say – are those expectations

## Caution: go-slow area ahead

so unreasonable? Not in themselves, certainly. Yet in reality, as I attempted to demonstrate in Chapter 3 when looking at various therapeutic approaches and their goals, any notions of absolutes or states of permanent and immutable happiness or psychic well-being are as misleading as they are unrealistic. In the most simplistic terms, what we can do is to help clients gain insight into the fact that they do have choices and can therefore take control of their lives, and to facilitate them in taking practical steps to carry that through – *but we cannot do it for them*.

This very basic notion can help to lift feelings of having to 'perform' and produce results. Following on from this, it is useful in taking the pressure off oneself to think of therapy not as a unilateral mission of investigation and analysis by the therapist, but a joint voyage of discovery in which therapist and client are co-navigators.

This is underlined by Patrick Casement (1995: 26) in a passage that also attests to the importance of tolerating states of un-knowing:

> *The therapist's openness to the unknown in the patient leaves more room for the patient to contribute to any subsequent knowing; and what is thus jointly discovered has a freshness which belongs to both. More than this, it may be that a significant part of the process of therapeutic gain is achieved through the patient coming to recognize that the therapist can learn from him or her. The patient is thus given a real part to play in helping the therapist to help the patient and, to that end, to discover what is needed in that patient's therapy.*

It is, of course, quintessentially human to feel anxious and impotent when faced with uncertainty and apparent impasse, especially when everything the world outside therapy throws at us indicates a wish for rapid-fire results and achievement. Even though those involved in brief therapy, cognitive behavioural therapy and modalities such as CAT (Cognitive Analytical Therapy), where one of the central tenets of the work is to be challenging and confront the client, will probably not agree, I believe that in therapeutically frustrating situations the only course of action is inaction. In other words, staying with the process, listening and making internal notes, and allowing things to develop.

I recall being put firmly on the spot in my first clinical encounter at my first placement, in a student counselling unit at a university. The young man in question had been coming to see me for some half a dozen sessions and I had bumbled and fumbled my way through them without having any real sense of what I was doing (some might say that experienced practitioners never entirely lose that feeling).

## On training to be a therapist

In about the sixth session he handed me a large book and said 'Have you read this? You should do'. It was one of those typical American blockbusters on personal development and was entitled *Unlimited Power And How To Acquire It*.

As you can imagine, my supervisor and my fellow supervisee had a field day with this cleverly orchestrated display of 'unlimited power' by the client, which only added to my discomfiture. I simply had not known how to react to the incident with the book, and left the session feeling like a small schoolboy who is hauled out in front of the entire school in assembly and given a dressing down by the headmaster. Looking back, I realize that my angst was really about what I saw as the deconstruction of my therapeutic persona. In other words, I felt I had lost my aura of competence and hence my credibility – if you like, my 'image' as a therapist. These qualities can seem overwhelmingly important to us when we are training, especially in the early stages, but what we can gradually come to realize is that we do not have to be a therapeutic version of Superman or Superwoman, nor do we have to attempt to appear that way. This is covered by Zaro, Barach, Nedelman and Dreiblatt (1978: 8):

> Some students react to the fears of being perceived as incompetent by attempting to bluff their way through the session by 'acting like a therapist' (e.g., by acting distant, authoritative, and uncommunicative). Others may reveal their insecurity or lack of knowledge to the client and try to promote a buddy relationship. It is often helpful to remember that two of the most common obstacles to learning to be a therapist result from preconceptions students may have with regard to how they should appear and from the fear of looking incompetent.
>
> Most new therapists find it difficult to accept the fact that they do not need to provide an answer for every question, that they do not have to respond immediately to everything the client presents. It is quite legitimate, even wise, to take time to think about your response to an issue and consult with your supervisor about it.

This is sound advice in principle, but in practice it can seem difficult or even impossible for students suffering from spiralling self-doubt to put these self-help concepts into practice. It is absolutely normal for trainees to feel they have to cloak themselves in an aura of therapeutic impregnability and to present an image, both in terms of their physical presence (which includes such things as dress and manner) and their intellectual and clinical prowess, which will make them acceptable to the client. In a sense, these feelings are something we all have to go

102

## Caution: go-slow area ahead

through, almost like a rite of passage, in order to get to the other side where we feel free to drop the various masks or false selves we have donned and to be our true selves without fear of being 'found out'.

The feeling that we have to 'do it right', whatever that may involve, is a powerful inhibitor for students. Fears of being judged and seen as incompetent can put us through the most unnerving and debilitating bouts of agony, soul searching and indecision, especially in the early stages of training when feelings of infantilization and self-consciousness can run riot. A typically angst-ridden 'pot-pourri' of feelings felt before a first ever session with a client are engagingly described by one trainee psychotherapist, Stefano Ferraiolo:

> I was sitting in the counselling room. It was my first client and I was so proud, but concerned at the same time. I was proud and delighted that having been in training for a few years, here I was, in a hospital fulfilling my dream of supporting people . . . The reason I was concerned was because I felt a complete novice and there was so much theory I needed to come to terms with and digest.
>
> Suddenly this theory was fast-forwarding inside my head. For a moment, I had the hallucinatory hope that all the relevant supporting themes that could make the session successful would be automatically selected and emphasized in my mind, as if by pure magic. It felt like being minutes away from taking an important examination. I dreamt about owning all the books I had ever come across and how they would automatically come to my rescue at the required moment if I required them to do so.
>
> I was a little nervous but serene at the same time. I felt ready to start. I had flicked through the assessment notes again and I felt confident. A reluctant nurse cleaned the room on my insistence; I also helped in this process. It was just 10 minutes before the time. Was this stating my need to create a nice and caring atmosphere? Only five minutes were left to the commencement of the session and I had spent the previous half hour setting up the frame. I had arranged the three chairs in the room, leaving the client to choose where to sit. Two chairs were on one side of the room and one faced the other two. Wherever the patient decided to sit I would be able to check the clock on the wall . . .
>
> Everything was set. Would she be on time? I would certainly be disappointed if she were late, however possibly relieved. If she were to be just a few minutes late, then the session would be shorter and I would have less opportunity of messing up. I still hoped that she was on time. It suddenly occurred to me that I would have felt almost relieved if she did not show up at all.

103

## On training to be a therapist

*It was interesting to reflect at a later stage on the contradictory set of emotions I was going through. At this stage, relating to any specific theory proved practically an impossible task regardless of the effort I made.*

When we are consumed by anxiety, even the smallest deviation from the expected therapeutic script can be overwhelming. Patients are supposed to adhere to a nice neat formula, as laid down for us in lectures and textbooks. They are not supposed to veer off at a tangent and come up with material or actions that we could not have anticipated. If we plan a session with meticulous detail, as Ferraiolo did in the example above with his carefully-placed chairs, any extraneous activity by the patient can be paralyzing. Whilst it is quite normal in early clinical encounters to try to cover all the angles and every possible scenario, that is quite simply setting oneself up for a fall. As I tried to drum into my eldest son when teaching him to drive, expect the unexpected – you will hopefully be less thrown by it when it comes, as it inevitably will.

Having said this, being on guard does not necessarily mean being able to deal with these therapeutic 'bombshells' when they suddenly appear, as I can personally confirm. In the middle of a somewhat fraught session, one of my first clients, another young student at the university where I had my placement, suddenly tossed me a charming little hand-grenade when she asked me: 'What exactly are you – a psychologist, a psychiatrist, a counsellor, or what? And what's your orientation?'

Panicking like crazy, I sat there stone-faced and resisted the temptation to tell all. 'I'm just a pathetic little trainee. My orientation is the "make-it-up-as-you-go-along-and-pray-it-works" school', I wanted to confess. 'Please don't be too hard on me. I'll get enough stick from my supervisor as it is. Just stay with me for a few more sessions, please. I need you.' With all this going through my mind, I simply mumbled something about being a counsellor, tried to cover up my blushes by pretending I was having a coughing fit, and just prayed she would not probe any more.

On occasions, one's worst fears can become reality, as Grainne Hashemi, a qualified counsellor, recalls in an amusing account of a first-ever session with a client:

*I was doing my placement at a youth counselling centre. My first client was a 19-year-old male. It all got off to a bad start when I went into the wrong room and interrupted a colleague of mine mid-session. Then my client arrived 15 minutes late. By this stage*

**104**

## Caution: go-slow area ahead

*I was such a nervous wreck that I couldn't even get my words out.
I had 'you are my first client' in large letters on my forehead. I
think he was quite amused by this and began by asking where I
had got my trousers. He said they were really nice and he wanted
a pair. I just stared at him in disbelief, thinking 'what the hell do
I say at this point?' He then told me about a club he had been
to at the weekend and before I had the chance to say anything remotely intelligent, he stood up and said 'Sorry, I have to go now'
and walked calmly out the door.*

One practical question we must consider is whether to
'own up' to clients about being a trainee (the subject of self-disclosure
by therapists is dealt with more fully in Chapter 7). Some institutions
make it easy on trainees by insisting they are up-front about their status
from the start; others suggest a frank disclosure when the subject arises
in a session; whilst there are some who feel it is better left unsaid,
preferring to use the opportunity to question why the client feels it
important to know about such things. My personal view is that honesty
is the best policy up to a point. In other words, we should admit to being
in training when the client asks to know and, whilst it can be valuable
to look at what this means for the client, it is arguably far more important to analyse and work through what kind of implications our 'learner'
status has for us.

In this context, we should try to focus on what qualities
we have, rather than those we do not have. To explain this further, it
can be all too easy to become weighed down by feelings of inadequacy,
whether clinical or academic or both, especially when we compare ourselves to tutors, supervisors and fellow trainees. However, the fact that
they appear to have more knowledge and experience should not be
allowed to detract from our own unique qualities and experience, as
underlined by Abrahao Brafman (1999: 18):

*Your normal self-criticism and your presumably long-held idea of
what a therapist is supposed to do are bound to make you deride
most of the possible interventions that come to your mind. Being a
student of a new discipline tends to make you oblivious of the value
that experience in other fields (including your own life!) has in
enabling you to understand this person now turning to you for help.*

Taking this a step further, Theodor Reik (1998: 145–7) not
only advocates relying on one's own instincts, he also actively discour-
ages young analysts from relying too heavily on accepted wisdom:

**105**

## On training to be a therapist

*Young analysts should be encouraged to rely on a series of most delicate communications when they collect their impressions; to extend their feelers, to seize the secret messages that go from one unconscious to another. To trust these messages, to be ready to participate in all flights and flings of one's imagination, not to be afraid of one's own sensitivities, is necessary not only in the beginnings of analysis; it remains necessary and important throughout . . .*

*The student of psychoanalysis is advised to listen to those inner voices with more attention than to what 'reason' tells about the unconscious; to be very aware of what is said inside himself . . . and to shut his ear to the noises of adult wisdom, well-considered opinion, conscious judgement. The night reveals to the wanderer things that are hidden by day.*

The question we need to ask ourselves when we are gripped by these negative, self-critical feelings is what exactly we are afraid of, and what do we perceive as the possible consequences of that fear. I believe that in many cases our anxiety and consequent need to 'get it right' at all times, is not only linked to our self-esteem, and more practical worries about being judged by course leaders, but is also born out of a belief that it is potentially inimical, or even fatal, to the therapeutic process to make a mistake. That may well be true in some cases, but before we accept this as an immutable fact we need to look at the whole concept of error in therapeutic terms and to realize that, given the ineffable and very individual nature of therapy and each separate therapeutic encounter, the majority of these 'mistakes' are not mistakes at all in the accepted sense of the word.

Before debating the ramifications of so-called therapists' mistakes, it is first essential to define what is meant by a mistake in therapeutic terms. I believe that above all else it is the therapeutic relationship – and the working alliance that stems from that relationship – that is crucial to the client's psychic growth and well-being. Therefore, anything that damages that relationship and alliance by lessening the client's trust or his feeling of being contained, held, empathized with and understood, could be classed as a mistake. If the damage cannot be properly repaired, it is what might be termed a mistake of the 'malignant' kind, that is to say one that will eat away at the therapeutic relationship like a cancer. This is in contrast to a 'benign' error which can be worked with and, in many cases, may actually benefit the relationship by increasing trust and understanding.

Classical psychoanalysts, amongst others, would argue against the view that the relationship between therapist and patient is

## Caution: go-slow area ahead

the sine qua non of successful therapy. They would maintain that resolution of the transference is the cornerstone of all meaningful therapeutic work. This means they would highlight the fact that the client's relationship with the therapist is a distorted one based on a previous relationship in the client's life and is therefore reflective of how they relate to others in the world outside the consulting room (the subject of transference is dealt with more fully in Chapter 7). Psychoanalysts would also place great emphasis on using interpretation to bring the unconscious into consciousness, which would include transference interpretations.

There is no room in this book for a full justification of the belief that the therapeutic relationship is the key factor in therapeutic effectiveness. However, it would be fair to say that there is amongst most schools, even psychoanalysis, a growing acceptance for at least some espousal of the basic principle. Writing in the *International Journal of Psychoanalysis* (1998: 904), Daniel Stern, Louis Sander, Jeremy Nahum *et al.* come to the conclusion that:

> *There has long been a consensus that something more than interpretation, in the sense of making the unconscious conscious, is needed . . . Anecdotal evidence suggests that after most patients have completed a successful treatment, they tend to remember two kinds of nodal events that they believe changed them. One concerns the key interpretation(s) that rearranged their intrapsychic landscape. The other concerns special moments of authentic person-to-person relationship . . . with the therapist that altered the relationship with him or her and thereby the patient's sense of himself. These reports suggest that many therapies fail or are terminated not because of incorrect or unaccepted interpretations, but because of missed opportunities for a meaningful connection between two people.*

Petrūska Clarkson (1999: 34 and 147) is more explicit on the therapeutic or working alliance:

> *A well-functioning psychotherapeutic alliance is a basic precondition which is rarely taken into account when it exists and yet can undermine the quality of the psychotherapy more seriously than anything else if disturbed . . . According to most researchers, as reviewed by Gelso and Carter (1985), the importance of the working alliance is significant in most if not all psychotherapeutic approaches . . .*
>
> *Research has shown that it is important for the client that there be a real relationship from within which matrix the psychotherapist may use whatever theory or technique he or she espouses.*

107

## On training to be a therapist

*Theoretical orientation consistently seems to be far less important to clients than the experienced value of a real relationship – right from the beginning of psychotherapy.*

Given that the relationship between therapist and client is so vital to the process, let us look first at the kinds of actions, suggestions or interpretations by the therapist that can be classed as sufficiently inappropriate or damaging to qualify as malignant mistakes that will eat away at and eventually destroy that relationship. Transgressions of basic human rights and laws, such as murder and physical abuse, and sexual relations whilst therapy is ongoing (there is much debate about such relations subsequent to therapy) would appear to fall into the unacceptable category, as would unreliability by a therapist (i.e. consistent lateness or non-attendance), total lack of empathy, being overtly judgemental, and attempting to impose one's own values or ways of thinking and being on the client.

In its document, *Ethical Requirements for Member Organisations*, section 2.5, entitled 'Relationship with Clients', the United Kingdom Council for Psychotherapy (2000) briefly summarizes what it regards as unacceptable therapist behaviour by stating: 'Psychotherapists are required to maintain appropriate boundaries with their clients. They must take care not to exploit their clients, current or past, in any way, financially, sexually or emotionally.'

These categories might appear to be self-evident, but they could be seen as open to many different interpretations. For example, the idea of what constitutes sexual exploitation of clients can differ wildly. In a highly controversial case study, Brian Thorne, the distinguished author and therapist, relates how he treated the sexually frigid wife of a fellow Christian in a manner that would surely be regarded as going far beyond the pale by most practitioners whatever their orientation, and could be seen as a gross abuse of power by the general public.

Thorne describes in some detail how he engaged in touching, caressing and embracing his colleague's wife when they were both naked and he was sexually aroused. He writes (1991: 96):

> It was possible for us both to be naked and vulnerable before each other and to discover that our bodies and our sexuality were trustworthy and that our desiring was in harmony and not in conflict with our ethical selves.

Many would question Thorne's use of the word 'ethical' even though he had the consent and full cooperation of both his client and her husband for this unconventional treatment process. Indeed,

**108**

## Caution: go-slow area ahead

Thorne admits his own concerns about how the therapy could be perceived, stating at one point '... there was a strong sense in both of us ... that what we were doing could be perceived as illicit, disreputable, even sinful' (1991: 90). Bearing in mind the overtly sexual nature of the therapy, as attested to by Thorne's arousal, it surely cannot be condoned if only because it would set the most dangerous precedent.

Having said that, it is arguably difficult to class Thorne's behaviour as a malignant mistake in categorical terms because there is no evidence that the therapy damaged the client in any way. Quite the opposite, according to Thorne, who states that at the end of therapy the client was able to resume full sexual relations with her husband after years of frigidity. Given a satisfactory outcome from a client's point of view, even forms of behaviour that would usually fall outside the most basic ground rules could in theory be regarded as therapeutically justifiable.

It is my personal belief, however, that the end can never justify such extreme and unconventional means as those adopted by Thorne, even allowing for his client's positive affirmations. I would contend that at least one of the basic conditions that should be offered to clients as a prerequisite for therapy was compromised by the nature of the treatment. Michael Patton and Naomi Meara (1996: 348–50) refer to these conditions as 'virtues' and list them as: 'moral integrity, respectfulness, benevolence and prudence'.

If these virtues are adhered to and the therapeutic alliance is strong enough, anything which might otherwise be regarded as an error, such as deviations from the therapeutic frame perpetrated by the therapist (for example arriving late, changing a session time, or altering the fee), can usually be rectified and in many cases capitalized on – provided the therapist not only uses his skill to rebuild any ruptures in the alliance but also acknowledges his mistake. This is underpinned by Robert Langs (1998: 37), whose Communicative approach is based very much on the implications of frame management and mismanagement:

> The best that can be done under frame-modified conditions is to interpret properly the negative unconscious perceptions and symptomatic effects of the deviations involved and secure those deviations that prove to be unnecessary and uncorrectable. The healing qualities of this understanding and reframing are thereby pitted against the harmful effects of the remaining deviations. This is a difficult battle, but therapists who keep secured all aspects of a frame that can possibly be held secure, and who soundly interpret the patient's experience of the deviant aspects, are more likely to be deeply helpful than harmful.

## On training to be a therapist

I believe it is not humanly possible to be absolutely consistent, focused, and empathic towards our clients at all times. We are not, nor should we be, therapeutic automatons. Clients have to learn to come to terms with therapists who are ordinary, fallible human beings (this concept is examined in more detail in Chapter 7). Given that therapy is an intimate encounter between two people exploring the deepest, and often darkest, canyons of one person's mind, it is simply not feasible to carry out that work without deviating from textbook guidelines, and saying and doing things that might be regarded by some purists as errors.

Furthermore, it can be said that clients not only prefer therapists who show human frailty and unknowing, in some cases they unconsciously attempt to bring about therapist 'error' for their own purposes, a concept originally postulated by Donald Winnicott and helpfully explained by Michael Jacobs (1995a: 80–1) in his book about the great 'D.W.':

> What Winnicott . . . states is enough for some patients to get well is that 'in the end the patient uses the analyst's failures, often quite small ones', some of which will have been 'manoeuvred' by the patient. The key factor is that the patient is then able to hate the analyst for the failure, originally experienced in an early environmental failure, but now repeated in the transference. 'In the end we succeed by failing – failing the patient's way'.

Lewis Wolberg (1988: 797) offers a different slant on this famous piece of Winnicottian theory:

> At certain phases in treatment therapist improprieties may become more pronounced than at others. For instance, during periods of resistance the therapist may respond with aggressive or rejecting behaviour . . . The patient may be sensitive to the moods of the therapist and work on these for specific gains, the most insidious effect of which is a sabotaging of the treatment effort.

An example of this type of 'client-driven' error arose in my work with one of my first private clients, whom I will call Rosemary. She was a lawyer in her early 40s, extremely sharp and intelligent, and probably the most difficult and challenging individual with whom I have worked. Her opening question to me when she first telephoned was 'Are you good?' and set the tone for the therapy in terms of her ability to put me under constant pressure by belittling me, patronizing me and generally 'getting under my skin'.

**110**

### Caution: go-slow area ahead

Rosemary's abrasiveness and her need to knock me down was a manifestation of her own deep-seated insecurity and sense of worthlessness, which had been engendered principally by her mentally sadistic mother, who belittled and undermined her. This left her deeply fearful of developing intimate relationships in adulthood. She was convinced that if she got too close to other people they would perceive her as bad and unworthy.

Much of our early work centred around Rosemary's difficulty in allowing herself to acknowledge that there was a relationship between us at all, and, as the sessions wore on, her need to determine what the nature of that relationship was by constantly testing the boundaries. These issues reached a climax when, as a result of Rosemary goading me into responses which could be regarded (and were by my supervisor) as falling well outside the textbook kind of therapeutic intervention, she allowed her underlying fears to surface dramatically. My instinctive and uncharacteristic responses, based on countertransference feelings subconsciously engineered by Rosemary, left me fearing that I had irreparably damaged the therapy, but they did in fact lead to a new level of understanding developing between us.

In one particular session, some four months into our work, Rosemary became increasingly irritated and said that she felt she was not moving on and that nothing was happening in the therapy. She pursued this line for some while, suggesting that it was my job to set the agenda and the pace, and talking of her need to get value for money, a frequent theme of hers. I became overwhelmed by feelings of therapeutic impotence and a sense of being de-skilled. In what felt like desperation rather than careful reasoning, I suggested to her that she should consider the possibility that I might not be the right therapist for her.

My reaction seemed completely to take the wind out of Rosemary's sails. From appearing hectoring and overbearing, she suddenly became almost childlike in her protestations. She told me that she had heard my suggestion as a directive that she *should* find another therapist and that she had felt incredibly rejected by it. I pointed out to her that in my opinion she had unconsciously set the rejection up and that this reflected her own fear of being rejected in relationships, which she unconsciously sought to avoid by rejecting the other person first.

The crucial interchange was not finished by a long way. Rosemary then said she felt I would keep her on as a client purely because of the money and added that it was important for her to know that she was more than just a banknote to me. This elicited another defensive gut response from me which, even as I was saying it, I feared was not 'the right thing to do' in conventional terms. I told her that,

## On training to be a therapist

although I would not usually have said this to a client, I felt I needed to let her know that I did not work as a therapist because of the money.

My supervisor told me that my response was the very thing I should *not* have said. In his opinion Rosemary needed me to be a therapist at that moment and nothing else. I believe that in practical terms my supervisor was wrong for the simple reason that Rosemary's relationship with me clearly took an upward turn after I was forced into being human rather than technically correct. My errors could be regarded as benign rather than malignant because in the final analysis Rosemary was able to see me as a real person rather than a therapeutic automaton, a factor that was crucial in allowing her to work with me at a deeper level.

In retrospect, it is possible to argue that my responses to Rosemary were not merely off-the-cuff reactions; they were intentional and considered rejoinders, albeit via an unconscious process, to everything that had gone before. This scenario is well summarized by Bertram Pollens (1993: 105), who, reflecting on a similarly unconventional interaction with a patient, writes:

> *Even though this was a spontaneous emotional response on my part, it was made possible only by the fact that I had already studied and thought out the dynamics of this patient carefully on an intellectual level and made the image of his pathology a part of me.*

The ability to be 'real' in the relationship (see Chapter 4) is a key factor when looking at the issue of therapist error. Being real means being authentic or true to yourself in the face of pressures from theory and supervisors that, especially when we are trainees, can act as a therapeutic straitjacket. It is important to state, however, that this does not mean doing and saying whatever takes your fancy at the time. A broken bone, when healed, is often stronger than the original bone, but we must take great care not to allow bones to get broken in the first place.

Clients will very often forgive us for interpretations that are not correct, and technical errors such as frame disturbances, if these can be seen to be in some way arising from or connected to the immediacy of the therapeutic interaction and are the result of human fallibility. However, they will not take so kindly to errors that are the result of a rigid, tunnel-visioned therapeutic stance based purely on dogma and theory.

I believe the importance of being ourselves, whilst keeping within certain fundamental ethical parameters and theoretical guidelines (i.e. the code of conduct of an accrediting body such as the UKCP or BACP, and the framework of our core therapeutic model) cannot be overstated. If we think of therapy in this light, the whole concept of therapist error – serious transgressions apart – becomes nebulous and, to a certain extent, meaningless. This does not give us licence to do anything we feel like doing, but in terms of our self-critical feelings it can help to lessen the awful burden of having to 'get it right' in everything we say and do. As training progresses and we gain more clinical experience, we gradually develop internalized boundaries that help us instinctively to sense the difference between what is right and what is wrong in therapeutic terms.

No, we can never be perfect and nor should we aspire to be. Ironically, by developing the ability to 'hang loose' in clinical encounters we can be better therapists, more perceptive and more attentive to our clients needs. By focusing too much on ourselves and our fumblings and bumblings we merely hinder that development. This is something highlighted by Nina Coltart (1992: 103, original emphasis) in an observation that makes a fitting conclusion to this chapter. Coltart is talking of the danger of therapists falling into 'a maelstrom of guilt' as a result of error and says that this 'blocks clear thinking, and may well inhibit the analyst from an unselfconscious look at exactly how the patient is responding and what can and should be made of that'. She continues:

> Over the years, I have come to think that it is in itself a mistake to attach exaggerated power to **any one thing** that we say or do; from this overestimation can arise constricting and anxious fears, especially in the young analyst, about being 'destructive' to a patient or a treatment . . . Patients are in an exposed and dependent position; subtle ways in which they retain any power are not easily accessible to them; it is not our job to overemphasize their dependence or to strip them of realistic power, and it may well be that a recognition by them that the analyst can be wrong, or stupid, or know less than they do about various things, including themselves, may lead to beneficial results.

# 7     Up close and personal

Imagine the scene – or perhaps you would rather not. You emerge from the shower at your local health club naked as the day you were born, dripping with water, hair a soggy mess, to be confronted by the nightmarish apparition of one of your clients. As if that were not mortifying enough, the client seems intent on wringing every last drop of angst from the situation by engaging you in small talk, whilst at the same time looking you up and down with mild amusement, or perhaps pity. Meanwhile, you stand there like a rabbit frozen in the glare of a car headlights, hoping it is just a bad dream and that you will soon wake up safe and serene in the sanctity of your own therapist's couch.

Believe it or not, that was exactly what happened to one of my fellow trainees at my first placement after she had finished a workout at the campus gymnasium. My unfortunate colleague was so shocked by the unexpected encounter with her client that she stood there rooted to the spot, paralysed mentally and physically to the extent of being unable even to wrap a towel round herself to protect her modesty. She apparently managed to mumble something like 'Oh, hello. I didn't expect to meet you here. Do you come here often?' before stumbling away utterly traumatized.

This example of client shower power was apparently not a unique occurrence by any means. Brett Kahr, the writer and psychotherapist, who chaired a fascinating seminar at London's Tavistock Clinic on unplanned contact with clients, said he had heard of two or three

## Up close and personal

similar cases of therapists reduced to shivering wrecks by the sight of clients looming at them suddenly like Anthony Perkins' infamous shower murderer in Alfred Hitchcock's film, *Psycho*.

Kahr also reported the case of a therapist who joined a dating agency and went out filled with romantic expectations on his first date only to discover that the lady in question was one of his clients. Petrūska Clarkson (1999: 48) takes this a step further when she tells how a psychotherapist spending some time in a foreign country, decided to visit a sex shop and, as she was leaving, encountered the husband of a marital couple who had been in therapy with her back in England. The therapist, who was clearly a paragon of cool, calm collectedness, simply shook hands with the client and moved on unabashed.

Occasionally you come across a client who seems to home in on you like a guided missile wherever you go. I remember, in the university placement mentioned earlier, I was seeing a client who I seemed fated to meet in almost every conceivable situation – walking down the street, in my health club, shopping in the local supermarket, and even at the dentist. In the end, I hardly dared to venture from my house for fear of being assailed by her cheery 'Hello, fancy meeting you here' style of greeting. Happily they did not have mixed saunas at the health club or I would doubtless have been stripped of my defences forever.

It would be comforting if we could always deal with un-planned contact in the self-possessed manner of the therapist in the aforementioned sex shop encounter. The reality is, however, that such meetings can faze even the most experienced therapists, and for trainees they can evoke overwhelming feelings of anxiety and exposure. Based on the evidence of my student questionnaires, as well as some general research I conducted amongst trainees, the matter of unplanned contact with clients is one of the four most anxiety-producing issues for trainees in their work with clients. The others are: how to deal with direct questions from clients and the concomitant issue of whether to self-reveal; working with the relationship between therapist and client, using what are usually referred to as transference interpretations; and the whole area of sexuality in the consulting room. (I have focused here on more general issues and have therefore not included in this category students' concerns regarding working with particular types of clients such as borderline, suicidal, sexual abusers, anorexic/bulimic, etc.)

Beginning with the issue of unplanned contact, there is little point in students attempting to turn to the experts for guidance because, as was made patently clear at the Tavistock seminar, there is virtually nothing of consequence on the subject in the current literature. Indeed, it appears that nothing of real significance has been written

# On training to be a therapist

about unplanned contact since the days of Freud, who showed that the issue was clearly not a problem for him by regularly bumping into his patients on the streets of Vienna, socializing with them and even taking them on holiday with him.

Maintaining strict boundaries was, of course, impossible for a man of Freud's fame. Nowadays if a therapist puts themself in the public domain by dint of their professional status, for example by writing books or making television appearances or radio broadcasts, they are clearly exposing themself to a far greater possibility of unplanned contact because in therapeutic terms such contact is not confined to physical meetings. Merely seeing or thinking about your therapist – or client – in another setting can produce all kinds of feelings and fantasies.

For example, I was stunned to see a photograph of one of my clients in a national newspaper, accompanied by an article alluding to his former life as a minor celebrity, which he had never mentioned. From that point on, it became a juggling act between utilizing this unexpected communication to inform my thinking, whilst at the same time attempting to bracket the knowledge I had gained so it did not interfere with the ongoing work of the therapy.

Psychotherapy and counselling training courses can encourage unplanned contact to a certain extent because many lecturers, group facilitators and supervisors are also therapists, and some do not consider it inimical to therapeutic work to see trainees from their own training establishments. Mixing in the world of therapy as part of one's training or continuing professional development, for example going to seminars and workshops, also opens up the possibility of close encounters of the destabilizing kind, as does developing a private practice and having your consulting room sited not too far away from where you live. Then again, merely living as a normal human being will always hold out the prospect of the unexpected face-to-face outside the consulting room.

With this notion in mind there is clearly a need to think about how we will respond in these situations. Talking of the desirability of maintaining the frame at all times, Clarkson (1999: 48) writes:

> At the same time, I know that this is an impossible goal and that it is more important for therapists and clients to learn how to handle boundary breaks than for them to engage in some embarrassed denial of these, which often ends in neither of the parties being properly equipped to deal with the consequences.

Taking Clarkson's line, it would seem necessary to think about how we respond in a twofold way – first at the time of the unplanned meeting, and second how we deal with the issues raised by that unexpected contact in the session or sessions immediately following it. Some therapists spell out at the beginning of therapy, when they make the contract, exactly what they will do if they meet their clients outside the therapeutic setting, for example 'I will say "Hello" or "Good morning" but no more'. However, even this approach cannot prevent feelings and fantasies being engendered in the client based on the context in which the unscheduled meeting takes place. For example, if you were to be seen by a client at a restaurant with your wife or husband, there could be many different issues, such as envy, that might arise as a result of that 'sighting' by a client who has difficulties in the area of relationships. No amount of pre-planned strategy could eliminate those feelings, nor should it.

My own view is that we should respond in a natural and human way when these unscripted meetings take place. Having said that, it seems important that there should be limitations to this form of interaction. A cheery greeting, with possibly a very brief interchange, is probably as far as it should go. To take the exchange further, that is to engage in a prolonged dialogue, could be prejudicial to the therapeutic relationship as there would be a danger of transforming that relationship into a social one, which therapy palpably is not. This is because the potential benefits of therapy are based on the specialness or uniqueness of the relationship which make it so different from any ordinary, everyday interaction. Maintaining some form of boundaries also offers clients a feeling of safety, that is to say they know where they stand as regards the nature of the relationship.

Having argued that it is best to act naturally, this idea can seem utterly unrealistic and impossible when we are in training and confronted suddenly by the unnerving sight of a 'rogue' client on the loose. Difficult though it may be, we should try to avoid a tendency to panic, and attempt to see beyond the immediate situation. One of the tenets of systems theory, as formulated by the Austrian biologist, Ludwig von Bertalanffy in the 1930s, is that there have to be periods of turbulence or deconstruction in order for new growth to begin, and this can be the basis for any subsequent work around unplanned contact. The material brought up by the client as a result of meeting his or her therapist in a 'non-therapeutic' situation can produce rich veins of material because it can engender such strong emotions and fantasies, often based on transferential issues.

Before looking at the kinds of issues that might arise in subsequent sessions as a result of unplanned contact, it seems important to examine why there is so often a sense of panic when we meet our clients outside the consulting room. What we, as therapists, appear to be

## On training to be a therapist

defending against is the fear of being seen as ordinary human beings with normal bodily needs, functions and desires – and also to be seen spending the client's money. Maintaining strict therapeutic anonymity is regarded as a key factor for those who espouse the 'blank screen' model of classical psychoanalysis and the psychodynamic approach where total non-disclosure by the therapist is seen as paramount. The theory behind this therapeutic stance is that if the client is allowed to know personal details about the therapist it is seen as a potential block to the development of transferences and clients' fantasies about the therapist based on not-knowing.

However, this rigid way of thinking does not allow for the fact that we do shop at the supermarket and use the local gym and swimming pool, so we will almost inevitably meet clients in unplanned situations from time to time. If we tried to avoid all these situations we would never leave our homes or consulting rooms, unless it was pitch black or we were wearing a disguise. Some therapists apparently never take on clients who live within a certain radius of their practice, but even this does not preclude the possibility of meeting them on planes, at the theatre, at a concert, or for that matter anywhere else where human activity takes place. Far better surely to feel free to live life without restrictions and be prepared to work with the material this kind of 'extra-curricular' contact brings up.

One matter on which the panel of experts at the aforementioned Tavistock seminar were in agreement was that any unplanned meeting must be acknowledged as soon as possible after it happens. The exact timing of such a reference must be sensitively handled, however. If it is raised too soon it can increase the effect of the intrusion; too late and it can become overlaid with other meanings. A full and timely exploration of the impromptu meeting can minimize any potential damage, as evidenced by Karen Levy, a counsellor, who recalls a paralyzing encounter with a client during training:

> One of my placements involved working with children and parents. The trustees of the placement organized a charity exhibition of the children's art, which I was invited to attend. I arrived straight from work and dashed into the changing room to change into a cocktail dress. The children were getting into costumes which they were going to wear at the event and some of the mothers were helping them to get dressed. As I was putting on my dress I noticed one of my clients there helping her daughter get ready. She saw me and came over and zipped up my dress and said something like 'You look lovely'. I said 'Thank you very much', but I was squirming. I didn't like her touching me; I felt totally exposed. What

118

## Up close and personal

*made it worse was the fact that I was wearing an expensive dress and I knew she had very little money. Shortly afterwards we had a session and I felt I had to bring the incident up and explore her feelings. Once it was dealt with it felt better, although it took a while for me to put it behind me.*

Whether it is raised by the therapist or not, it will very probably surface in the client's material in some form or other, and it is important not to let this communication pass by without exploration. One of the most significant issues that can be raised is that of an encounter with limitations. In other words, the fact that the boundaries have been breached in such a disturbing way can highlight the limitations of life itself and the fact that we are time-limited creatures. If we see therapy as a microcosm of life, such matters as emotional pain, disruption and gratification can be evoked, and there can be a contrast between intimacy and separateness, that is to say coming together in therapy and then going separate ways.

Perhaps the whole issue of unplanned contact can be best looked at in terms of the boundaries around therapy not being perfect. Indeed, it is surely unrealistic and undesirable to expect them to be perfect, which brings in Winnicott's ubiquitous concept of 'good enough', which can be applied not just to the good enough mother, as Winnicott originally used it, but to the whole gamut of human interaction. The fact is that we as therapists can only work within our human constraints, and, in the final analysis, that might not be such a bad thing. Clients should ideally be allowed to deal with the issue of the 'human' therapist and can benefit from seeing us as fallible (see Chapter 6).

Metaphorical nakedness can, of course, be equally disturbing. Which brings us to the second major angst-producing area of client work raised by students, that of facing direct, personal questions from clients. In everyday life we generally deal with questions directed to us and about us as if they were no different from any other form of communication. Yet, in front of a client in a consulting room, the mere idea of being asked something about ourselves can leave us feeling as if we have been asked to remove every last item of our clothing and conduct the therapy 'in the buff'.

Many trainees live in fear of being found out, in other words that their clients will discover they are in still training and feel cheated at not having a qualified practitioner. As I mentioned in Chapter 6, many institutions have strict guidelines about disclosing that you are in training, either when therapy begins or when the client asks you directly. As therapy increasingly comes under the microscope, clients are quite justifiably becoming more discerning in their choice of therapist,

**119**

# On training to be a therapist

so in terms of working professionally it is a practical necessity to have a professional qualification or accreditation in place.

However, in terms of working with clients during our training, the anxiety provoked by fear of discovery usually has more to do with how we feel about ourselves, that is to say having an internal structure that enables us to function effectively and with relative confidence. A client may indeed prefer to see someone who is qualified, but as with most direct questions from clients there is invariably another question behind it, and in the case of qualifications it is usually the simple issue of whether or not you are capable of helping them.

Shawn Tower, a qualified counsellor recalls the difficulties she encountered during her early training when faced with questions about her experience:

> *During training, I feared mostly those awkward questions that related to my counselling experience, or more precisely, lack of it. I never felt very comfortable either telling or indeed not telling clients that I was 'in training'. If I did admit to the above, the client might well inquire further: 'So how many clients have you actually worked with so far?', to which I would respond: 'Well, um, you are the first, actually.' On the other hand, how ethically 'good-enough' was not telling. Not very.*
>
> *My supervisor advised me to approach direct questions that felt awkward by voicing first the client's unconscious anxieties in the transference. This was helpful because their unconscious fears that I might be inadequate or even harmful as a counsellor were mine as well and so addressing the above could clear the air for both of us. If the client was still uncomfortable after my interpretation, I felt I would have to offer a direct answer but usually such questions seemed to fade away naturally. I think this may be because clients felt understood and thus more assured of the deeper understanding they were seeking in the first place. If I could help them understand themselves better then my actual experience, or actual inexperience as it were, became less significant. That is not to say that experience is unimportant. It does help very much, but it is not everything.*

There are various ways of dealing with direct questions. One supervisor I worked with suggested that we should respond by saying, 'I will answer your question, but first I would like to look at why you asked it'. I regard this as somewhat unhelpful in that it is not a very 'human' response, and could be felt as unempathic. Another simply said 'I wonder where that question came from?' The second response tackles

**120**

## Up close and personal

the issue of what lies behind the question in a more empathic way and could help the client to examine any underlying fears or concerns. When faced with a question about qualifications it should be possible to provide an honest answer and at the same time link it to an examination of the client's feelings about working with someone who is technically not qualified.

Of course there are times when Freud's putative dictum 'Sometimes a cigar is just a cigar' must come into play. Clients do ask 'social' questions that are not necessarily imbued with a hidden meaning – though, as stated earlier, I believe most direct questions do carry an element of what might be termed secondary significance, or in some cases primary significance. So if a client asks 'Did you have a nice holiday?' it is arguably perfectly okay to answer 'Yes. Thank you for asking'. However, if he or she then goes on to inquire about your holiday destination, whether you visited the local discotheque, and what factor suntan cream you used, you can be reasonably sure they are seeking more than just a polite social response.

If there is one factor that above all else engenders fear and uncertainty in the face of clients' questions it is the thorny problem of giving away personal information about ourselves. As stated earlier, the lengths to which therapists will go to in order to conceal every last detail about themselves depends very much on their orientation. So, in contrast to psychoanalysts, who build their whole approach around the analyst remaining a blank screen, those of other persuasions are, in varying degrees, more laid back about revealing personal information.

It would be fair to say that most approaches agree that there should not be wholesale self-disclosure because that could mean the therapy would focus too much on the therapist rather than the client. However, getting too hung up on retaining one's therapeutic anonymity is not only questionable, but also impossible because however hard we try we cannot be totally inscrutable; we are human beings and we do have a presence within the consulting room. Try as we might to shroud ourselves in mystery in our therapeutic encounters, our clients have a remarkable facility for finding out about us, not just from our general demeanour and the material things that surround us, but also from the therapeutic interaction itself, especially the unconscious messages we send out.

Patrick Casement (1995: 58) puts it this way:

*Patients do not see the analyst as a blank screen. They scrutinize the analyst, who aims to remain inscrutable, and they find many clues to the nature of this person they are dealing with . . . Analysts and therapists often give away more about themselves than they*

**121**

## On training to be a therapist

*realize. They might not speak openly about themselves, and they can be careful about personal questions, but they do not remain a closed book to the patient. Like a child who watches the mother's face for signs of pleasure or indications of mood, patients listen for similar signs from the therapist and there are many available.*

The $64,000 question is whether self-disclosure matters. The simple answer would seem to be that one should only self-disclose if it is for the benefit of the client. Making that judgement is not easy, but perhaps the rule of thumb should be: if in doubt, don't do it.

I was faced with just such a decision when a client, whom I had seen only four times, asked me if I was a parent. Most of his problems centred around his family of origin and the abuse and neglect that he had been exposed to within that family unit. As a consequence he had enormous difficulties in relating to his wife and children. Immediately before his question to me he had been talking about his feelings of being a failure as a parent. In response to his question, I put it to him that maybe he would feel I could not empathize with him if I was not a parent. He replied that he would indeed feel that I could not fully understand his difficulties with his children if I had none of my own.

Having thought about it, I decided disclosure would benefit the client. After I informed him that I was a parent, he thanked me for telling him and said that he felt much better about talking those particular problems through with me. It could be said that I had denied him the chance to work through any feelings and fantasies he might have had about a therapist who was not a parent and any concomitant issues arising out of that. However, in my judgement – and it is very much an individual thing – my self-disclosure actually strengthened the therapeutic alliance.

Developing a strategy for dealing with questions is something that needs to be thought through carefully if we are to be able to offer the client the most helpful response. If we wanted the whole thing neatly packaged we could arguably do no better than follow the dictum of Erich Fromm. Even though some might regard his thinking on this issue as too rigid and overlaid with power issues, it surely has much to commend it because of its clarity and straightforwardness.

Fromm stresses that the therapeutic relationship should not be characterized by an atmosphere of polite conversation or small talk, but by directness. He writes (1998: 193):

> *The analyst should answer all questions about himself which are on public record and which the patient has a right to know – such as age, training, social origin. In others the patient would have to*

**122**

## Up close and personal

*show why he has a legitimate interest or whether he wants to reverse the situation and analyze the psychoanalyst (because of resistance, for instance).*

The issues discussed so far in this chapter have to do with how comfortable we feel about ourselves as therapists when the spotlight is turned on us rather than the client. This arguably happens to a greater or lesser extent at all times during therapy, but is felt to be much more concentrated and pressurizing, especially by trainees, within the specific contexts I am describing here. This theme runs through all four topics touched on in this chapter, the third one being the ability or the willingness of the therapist to work with and to interpret the relationship in the room. That is to say, to draw attention to what is transpiring between therapist and client in the interaction within the consulting room, so that the client can perceive how their way of relating to the therapist repeats stuck or sedimented ways of relating to others, often parental figures in their past or present life.

This phenomenon is usually referred to as transference. It originated as a key principle of psychoanalysis, although it has now become an accepted part of the terminology and thinking of other therapeutic approaches. In his *Critical Dictionary of Psychoanalysis*, Charles Rycroft (1995: 185) defines transference as:

> *1. The process by which a patient displaces on to his analyst feelings, ideas, etc., which derive from previous figures in his life; by which he relates to his analyst as though he were some former object in his life; . . . by which he endows the analyst with the significance of another, usually prior, object. 2. The state of mind produced by 1 in the patient. 3. Loosely, the patient's emotional attitude towards his analyst.*

The so-called 'resolution' of the transference, in other words, the client coming to see how they are using the therapist to maintain these rigid patterns of relating, has traditionally been seen as the cornerstone of psychoanalysis without which no significant work can take place. However, towards the end of his definition (1995: 187), Rycroft offers a rider which appears to draw attention to the narrowness of the traditional psychoanalytic approach:

> *Most accounts . . . assume that the therapeutic effects of analysis are largely due to the opportunity provided by it to resolve 'within the transference' conflicts dating from childhood and infancy, and attach little importance to novel aspects of the analytical relationship,*

**123**

## On training to be a therapist

*such as the encounter with a person who combines interest with non-possessiveness and whose insight into the patient is probably more articulate and possibly actually greater than that of the actual parents.*

The phenomenon of transference has been written about and analysed at great length by a vast array of writers and my own brief attempt to explore it here is based solely on the way it can be used and dealt with by trainees in order to assist them in their understanding of clients' difficulties. Transference is often regarded by trainees as an extremely difficult concept to 'get one's head round' and to work with, and because of that it can be seen as something of a no-go area in the early stages of training. However, it is my belief that transference is not only a vitally important aspect of therapeutic work, but is in fact such a commonplace and everyday matter that it is actually far less complicated and hard to work with than trainees frequently perceive it to be.

I believe transference happens constantly in our interactions with others, in every area of life. Whenever we meet someone we form an opinion, a judgement or feelings about that person, and that opinion is often based, at least partly, on this person reminding us of someone with whom we had a prior relationship. To put it another way, the memory of a figure from the past is transferred onto the person we are now encountering. Even a name can induce transference feelings by, for example, making us think of that horrible aggressive little boy of the same name we knew when we were younger. Similarly, something as seemingly insignificant as the colour of someone's hair could have the same effect, for example I feel threatened by this person with the red hair because he reminds me of that red-haired bully at school. And, of course, this kind of relating happens all the time in sexual or romantic relationships where one partner is unconsciously perceived by the other as being like one of his or her parents, which may be the reason why they were attracted to them in the first place.

If we think of transference in these simple, everyday terms it can help us to understand how it operates within the consulting room. Michael Jacobs (1996: 96) puts it this way:

> *Most relationships are far from simple. They contain conscious and unconscious elements; they combine realistic perceptions of others, with exaggerated and distorted images of them based more on earlier relationships than on the present one. Perhaps we are never really sure that we relate to others as they actually are.*

A client faced with a therapist he has never met and about whom he knows virtually nothing in personal terms is bound to develop feelings or perceptions about that therapist, indeed it would be impossible not to do so. These feelings may be immediate or they may develop over time as the client unconsciously finds himself responding to the therapist in a manner that is often, but not always, based on a previous way of relating. An obvious example would be a client treating the therapist with undue deference and timidity based on the fact that they are seeing a distorted view of the therapist as their distant, authoritarian, emotionally withholding father or mother. In all probability such a client will treat other people in their current life, whom they see as authority figures, in the same overly deferential way.

In this context, the so-called 'triangle of insight' can be a helpful aid to thinking. Using this concept, the therapist draws attention to the fact that the client's way of relating to the therapist is based on their way of relating to a figure in their past life (such as a parent), and also reflects how they are relating to others in their current world outside the consulting room (as in my example above about authority figures). What is often emphasized is the 'as if' quality of the relationship, that is to say, for example, that the client is relating to you *as if* you were his father. This type of interpretation can be extremely powerful when it is handled sensitively and with correct timing because it demonstrates to the client in a highly relevant and accessible way the unconscious or stuck patterns of relating into which they have fallen.

The problem is that we often feel far too self-conscious to bring ourselves into the equation in such an obvious way. Indeed, bringing oneself into the picture by saying something like 'Perhaps you are seeing me as intrusive like your father' can feel embarrassingly self-centred and phoney. This perception is underlined by an early experience of one trainee, Frances Hillier:

> I was in the early stages of a psychodynamic training and my supervisor kept badgering me to make transference interpretations, which he said were absolutely crucial to the work. I remember trying desperately to spot any kind of opening which would allow me to bring myself into it, but they all seemed so false and contrived. Every time I even thought about it, it felt stupid and egotistical. When I finally did manage to say something about the client viewing me as being like her uncaring mother, I felt she was looking at me as if I was mad and thinking 'Why on earth are you talking about you? What have you got to do with anything?' In the heat of the moment I felt she was right – what on earth was I doing bringing myself into the picture like that? I felt ridiculous and incredibly self-conscious, but the funny thing was that she later admitted that I did remind her of her mother because I

**125**

# On training to be a therapist

*seemed so detached and business-like, so I guess my interpretation
did have the desired effect. However, it took me a long time to feel
even vaguely comfortable about doing it on a regular basis.*

Hillier's use of the word 'contrived' brings me back to a
point I made earlier regarding the fact that any transference interpretations need to be handled with sensitivity and made at the right time. If
they are not made in this way, and are made speculatively, or because it
is felt that one's theoretical approach demands it, then they *will* feel
contrived and will be perceived by the client as unhelpful, irrelevant or
even crass. The essence of successful transference interpretations is that
they must be based firmly in the reality of the situation in the consulting
room; in other words, the therapist must be as certain as he can be that
the client is relating to him in a transferential way based on a previous
relationship, so the therapist can therefore quite clearly see the parallels.
As with many clinical matters of this nature, the rule should be – if in
doubt refrain from doing it, or at least hold back until you are convinced
about why you are doing it.

It is my belief that some clients can be helped by being told
how transference works – indeed, some *need* to have it explained to
them. In general, I try to explain to clients as much as possible about
how therapy works rather than keeping the whole business as some sort
of mystical process, because I believe that as therapists we can take too
much for granted. With transference there are those who understand
the principle straight away and do not therefore need to be educated in
this way, but others find the concept strange and difficult to grasp at
first, and they therefore benefit from being taken through the theoretical aspect and then having this related to their own transferential material. I have experienced clients enjoying a real rush of insight when they
suddenly 'see the light' in terms of their transference(s).

Here again, Jacobs (1996: 100) is instructive: 'The decision
to draw attention to the transference needs to be a considered one . . . The
so-called resolution of the transference takes place through the client
coming to understand (partly intellectually, partly experientially) what
transference is.'

As an example of determining when to make transference
interpretations, I will briefly mention one of my first private clients, a
young man whom I will call Benny. Not long after I started seeing him,
Benny started coming late to our sessions on a regular basis. He then
twice negotiated a change in the session time, ostensibly because of
travel difficulties. I went along with his requests, but it meant considerable juggling on my part, and we eventually settled on a time very late
in the evening when I would not normally have worked. He also asked

126

# Up close and personal

me if he could come once a fortnight instead of once a week, which I told him I could not agree to because I could not hold a slot open on a fortnightly basis. I also told him that, in my opinion, once a week was the minimum necessary to obtain any benefit from therapy because a bigger gap between sessions would dilute the ongoing effect of the work.

Soon after this, Benny said he was finding it difficult to make ends meet and asked if I would consider a reduction in my fee. I explored this with him and, knowing he had problems with self-esteem, I suggested that before we agreed a reduction he should think about whether he was able to value himself enough to continue paying a full fee. However, he insisted that money was a huge problem for him and I eventually agreed to a reduction in my fee until he was able to get himself back on a sound financial footing, at which time, it was agreed, we would renegotiate.

Virtually every time Benny arrived for his session he would make some remark about dragging me out at some unearthly hour and asked if I minded being inconvenienced in this way. He said he was sure that I was not happy at having to be there at that time just for him. As the work progressed he revealed a series of disclosures about being let down or abandoned by significant others in his life. His father had abandoned him at quite an early age after divorcing his mother, who died soon afterwards, and he had then remarried an extremely possessive woman.

Benny's sister, whom he adored, and who had been largely responsible for bringing him up after losing their parents, went off to live in South America when Benny was a teenager and had severed all contact with him. He also had virtually no contact with his brother, who lived a considerable distance away from him. He also talked about a series of broken romantic relationships, which were apparently ended suddenly and painfully by his erstwhile partners in every case.

Suddenly I was struck by a revelation of what was going on between us. As Benny continued to express concern about inconveniencing me, I put it to him that because all the important people in his life had abandoned him, he was expecting me to abandon him, too. That was why he was so worried about what he perceived as dragging me out at such an inconvenient time. I suggested that he had in fact set up a potential rejection with me by constantly seeking to change the boundaries of our relationship, in other words messing me about so I would become fed up with him. I put it to him that he also did the same thing with other people with whom he was in relationship in any significant way.

Benny clearly found this very enlightening. He admitted that he had been living in constant fear that I would reject him by ending our sessions. He said that he believed I would not want to go on seeing him because of the inconvenient time and also because of the reduced fee, which he felt I would resent. Benny was then able to see how he set up similar rejections with other people in his current life based on his early experiences of abandonment and his expectation that this would be repeated forever. He said that because of this expectation he had deliberately made me 'jump through hoops' to test my commitment.

At that stage of my professional life, I was still not overly confident with transference interpretations and tended to hold back even when I sensed that transferential issues were being played out. It was only because I experienced Benny's unconscious manipulations in such a powerful and obvious way, within the immediacy of our relationship, that I was able to feel fairly certain of what was happening and was able to find the confidence to link his way of interacting with me to his past experiences in a way that was transformational.

As Rycroft suggested in his definition quoted earlier in this section, we must be careful not to allow a preoccupation with transference to obscure what is actually going on between therapist and client in the here and now. To see everything through the distorted lens of transference can lead to a situation where the therapist is the all-seeing adult and the client is stuck in some regressive, childlike way of being, which not only pathologizes everything the client says or does, but also totally denies what is happening in the room, i.e. the current interaction between two adults who are both engaged in a process of exploration. 'Bringing it into the room', as this therapeutic procedure is often termed, is essentially about acknowledging and working with feelings engendered in the client by the therapist which have a bearing on the client's current problems, especially his way of relating to others. This applies whether those feelings are a legacy from the past or are purely confined to the present.

If we pursue this theme of focusing on and working with the therapist–client relationship, it leads us to a potential situation that can be said to be glaringly obvious but which is frequently denied or dismissed because of the unease it engenders. The simple fact is that if you put two people alone in a consulting room in a situation where one is divulging their most intimate secrets, thoughts and desires, it is inevitable that in certain cases some form of attraction or attachment will develop, often based on prior encounters. There are, of course, occasions when there will be attraction, unilateral or mutual, which is based not on a throwback to the past, but on a simple chemistry between two people. But whether it is based on transference or the reality of the current situation, the issue of sexual attraction in therapy is one that cannot be downplayed or ignored simply because it feels so difficult to address – quite the contrary.

## Up close and personal

Sexuality within the consulting room, or as it is often re-ferred to, erotic transference and countertransference, forms the basis of the last of the four 'big issues' which trainees frequently find most uncomfortable and difficult to deal with. Indeed, sexuality can be de-scribed as a therapeutic 'hot potato' that can faze the most experienced practitioner, and can leave even the most competent and 'together' trainee experiencing hot flushes that have nothing to do with the onset of the (male or female) menopause.

Trainees' difficulties with sexuality was one of the topics addressed by Diane Rees-Roberts, a tutor and supervisor at Westminster Pastoral Foundation, during my interview with her for this book. Rees-Roberts said:

> *The whole area of sexuality is very difficult for trainees. In theor-etical terms it is fine, but when two people are together in a room it is quite different. Students can find it so hard to confront the erotic transference and interpret it to the client, in contrast to reading about it or discussing the subject in college. Also, it can be said that if there is a lack of erotic feeling, perhaps that is some-thing to talk about as well.*

Rees-Roberts' last point is particularly challenging because the first thing to accept when we are skirting around this awkward topic is that we are flesh and blood and therefore do experience both sides of the sexual coin; that is, clients can and do find us attractive and we are often attracted to clients. Elizabeth Morris (1996: 100) addresses the im-portance of acknowledging sexuality for the benefit of therapist and client:

> *The distinctions between 'being sexual', 'owning one's sexuality', and the extent to which we turn our conscious or unconscious awareness to this aspect, I think, are areas for individuals to pon-der on in relation to themselves. In the psychotherapeutic/personal development world segments of our humanness such as 'sexual-ity', 'personal power', 'wildness', have been highlighted as if they have a separate life of their own in order to help people focus on them . . . In the counselling room I think responding with an aware-ness of our own multi-facetedness is an asset and likely to serve a client well, so any withdrawal of awareness from our sexuality could dull the richness of our response.*

I remember when I obtained my first placement it seemed as if those in charge of the counselling unit were intent on giving me a trial by fire, because almost every student client I was referred seemed to be female and attractive. At one point I even had fantasies that I was being secretly observed by my supervisor to gauge my reaction. Having begun to put my paranoia into some kind of perspective, I then found myself feeling especially drawn to one young lady, whom I will call Amy, who began attending for therapy on a regular basis.

When I realized I was attracted to Amy in a more than superficial way, I became panic-stricken and the paranoia returned with a vengeance. I imagined that my placement would be revoked and I even feared that I would be 'struck off', like a doctor who acts in an unprofessional way towards a patient. I was so anxious about my feelings of attraction to this young lady that I took them to my own therapy and my therapist suggested I should have no hesitation in mentioning it to my supervisor.

Fearing the worst, I confessed all to my supervisor at the next supervision session. He smiled benignly and said something like: 'So? You're human aren't you. Let's look at *why* you're feeling this way. Is there something about her that *invites* you to feel attracted by her, or sexually stimulated? It might give us a clue as to how she relates to men in general.' What my supervisor was suggesting was that perhaps Amy was acting in a seductive manner because that was her habitual way of relating to men based on earlier experiences that made her feel she had to act that way.

After inwardly sighing with relief at my supervisor's reaction, I began thinking the situation through and focused on Amy's demeanour and the kind of material she brought to our sessions. On reflection, she did indeed present herself in a seductive way, often wearing sexy, revealing outfits. Furthermore, she made no secret of the fact that she had been involved in a series of 'one-night stand' encounters with men. Following my supervisor's lead, I was careful to listen over the next few weeks for any material from the past that might explain her overt sexuality now.

Eventually, some two or three months later, she revealed that she had been abused by a close relative when she was about 14 years old, and that her father, who was distant and unloving, had indulged in a string of brief affairs, which he flaunted in front of her. With the help of my supervisor, I was able to make Amy see that she both expected and invited men to take advantage of her sexually. Her perception was that sexuality equated to getting attention and affection; this was how she rationalized the fact that her father preferred his lovers to her. Giving herself sexually was the only way she felt she could get any affection or attention from men, including me. The intimacy and closeness she felt in those one-night stands, though appallingly brief and one-sided, was, for her, better than nothing.

## Up close and personal

Of course, it may happen that clients will be attracted to their therapist because quite simply they find him or her desirable, not because they are a representation of a figure from the past. This could be because of straightforward physical attraction, or it might be because the client feels drawn to the attentive, empathic nature of the therapist in the way patients traditionally 'fall in love' with their doctor or nurse. But, a note of caution for trainee therapists who feel flattered when they become the apparent love object of a client – the client's desire is probably not what it appears to be.

I remember a tutor on one of my courses giving a wonderful, self-deprecating exposition of this situation when he referred to being very obviously lusted after by a female client who was much younger than he was. My tutor explained it this way: 'When a middle-aged, balding man with a pot belly finds himself the object of desire for a highly attractive young lady client, you know you are in the presence of transference!'

Overt sexuality can be scary and unpleasant, especially when the client abuses the safety and confidentiality of the therapeutic situation. An anecdote from Lisa Steele, now a qualified therapist, illustrates this:

> When I began training, my very first patient was a gentleman in his late sixties who was having some psycho-sexual problems. I was very nervous when I went to meet him. He told me that with other therapists he had been used to sitting back to back as it made it easier for him to talk about his problems. Being inexperienced, I agreed, but I found it a very uncomfortable way of working; apart from anything else, it was difficult to hear what was being said. After supervision, I summoned the courage to tell him that if we were to continue working together we would have to sit with our chairs facing each other. He agreed to this and during the six months I saw him he continued to tell me how he acted out his sexual fantasies at home. However, instead of using characters from television soaps as stimulation, he would use me (I should have stayed back to back). This made for some very interesting work! It was a very complicated case for someone so inexperienced and was also very frightening.

Trainees are often reluctant to admit to any kind of sexual feeling in the room, especially in supervision, because they feel they might be judged or censored. Though entirely understandable, this is an unhelpful way of thinking, both for the trainee and for the client. As my example with Amy showed, looking for unconscious motivation, or reasons why the client is behaving seductively or is attracted to you as

**131**

therapist, is a good basis for dealing with the awkwardness that can arise in these situations.

Here again, we can enlist the help of Jacobs. He is looking at Fenichel's analysis of the narcissistic needs of hypersexual people (i.e. nymphomaniacs and Don Juans), and hysteric or schizoid ways of relating, but his comments could arguably be applied to all situations where sexuality rears its head within the consulting room. Jacobs writes (1995b: 106–7):

> *Sexuality is used as a substitute for a more primitive need, the wish to be reunited with mother; and the sexual greed which is often apparent is a substitute for infantile needs of love . . . the counsellor who encounters the 'hysteric' will also need to look for problems which run deeper than sexuality; considering the possibility that such a person is desperately unhappy, hungry for love, and yet terrified of rejection. The counsellor will then not be seduced by the excitement of the sexual presentation or repelled by her distaste of it.*

But what about when passion is real and not transferential? And what do we do when our own passion threatens to become uncontainable? If it is the client who is making the overtures, then if we have explored their feelings, as Jacobs suggests, and there is no obvious interpretation of a deeper motivation, we can only try to contain the situation. Another of my tutors stated explicitly to an obsessively amorous client that he was her therapist and not a potential lover. This seems overly harsh and unempathic and would not allow for exploration of the client's feelings, although if the client persisted and made it awkward for the therapist a terse response might be ultimately be necessary. When a client realizes his or her passion is unrequited, any subsequent work may revolve around feelings such as loss, frustration or anger.

The ethical aspect of therapists acting out their erotic countertransference and having sexual relations with their clients was discussed in Chapter 6 when dealing with therapist error. Suffice it to say at this point that whilst there is evidence showing that a surprising number of therapists would engage in sexual relations with clients if they felt it to be suitable (Clarkson 1999: 24), it cannot, in my opinion, be justified in any way, certainly not whilst therapy is ongoing at any rate. Such behaviour is an abuse of power, and it is based on an unequal relationship in terms of the therapist knowing far more about the client than the client knows about the therapist. Furthermore, if it becomes known about in a wider context or is seized on by the media, it leaves

## Up close and personal

the profession of therapy open to charges of abuse of power and general condemnation by the public at large.

The desire one feels for clients can be real and profound, but it is very often engendered purely by the intimacy of the therapeutic situation itself, rather like the situation mentioned earlier where a patient 'falls in love' with their nurse or doctor, only in reverse. In other words by the very act of caring for and nurturing the client, the therapist becomes emotionally connected to them. Our training may tell us that this is the last thing to which we should succumb, but all the theory and training in the world cannot take away our human frailty and foibles, and the fact is that this *does* happen.

The point I am trying to make here is that this kind of attachment to clients is almost invariably based on what might be termed an 'artificial' way of relating. It may well involve what are experienced as genuine feelings of attraction or even love on the part of the therapist, but if the relationship were transposed outside the consulting room the infatuation would, in most cases, be dissipated and the relationship would not be tenable without the bridge of the therapy.

David Mann's (1997) book, *Psychotherapy: An Erotic Relationship*, offers a psychoanalytic perspective on sexuality within the consulting room, but his frank exploration of this whole area has meaning for most therapeutic approaches. I offer three brief extracts from his work as a summation of why it is so important for trainees (and experienced practitioners) to be bold and 'think erotic'. In his introduction, Mann writes (1997: 1): 'To summarize this whole book in a single sentence: I consider that the erotic pervades most if not all psychoanalytic encounters and is largely a positive and transformational influence.'

Later in the book, Mann expands on this theme (1997: 9–10):

> *Consider this: it is my proposition that the emergence of the erotic transference signifies the patient's deepest wish for growth. Like those in love, patients wish to be known and understood, to change what they do not like about themselves, to alter what makes them unlovable. Through the erotic, light is shone on the deepest recesses of the psyche. The fundamental nature of the erotic is that it is psychically binding and connects individuals at the most intimate and deepest of levels.*

He continues (1997: 24):

> *What our patients need is the therapist's understanding in order to liberate the optimum range of their emotional experiences, so*

**133**

## On training to be a therapist

*that they can have more satisfactory and loving relationships out-side therapy . . . Unless it is experienced as a feeling or a passion, the erotic remains split off and distorted (note: not sublimated) into a highly intellectual activity that is no doubt interesting but is hardly transformative for either the patient or therapist. Love . . . is an inherent part of the analytic work. With adults, there is no love for another which is devoid of erotic fantasy.*

The focus of this chapter has been feelings engendered in trainees when they suddenly find themselves in the spotlight to a degree that feels uncomfortable or untenable. If we accept that the basis of any meaningful or transformational work is the therapeutic relationship or alliance, then it can be said that we are never out of the spotlight, nor should we be. Having also stressed that it is important for clients to accept a therapist with limitations, we must leave room for those unscripted twists and turns of the therapeutic plot that inevitably arise from time to time and which offer an opportunity to be creative and to demonstrate human responses. To quote one of the panellists at the Tavistock seminar on unplanned contact, perhaps in order to do this work properly we *need* to be seen naked in the shower.

# 8 The bitter-sweet taste of freedom

One of the more curious phenomena that appears to be manifesting itself increasingly as we head deeper into the new millennium is an addiction to addictions. Rather like the obsession with identifying different kinds of rages – road rage, computer rage, trolley rage, etc. – discovering and defining all kinds of new addictions has become almost fashionable, especially with the media who simply by naming a particular rage or addiction often appear to create it and give it life. Thus, in addition to the well-established addictions such as alcohol, drugs, cigarettes and gambling, we now have people addicted to sex, computers, computer games, the internet, television soaps, chocolate, mobile phones and numerous other weird and (not so?) wonderful features of modern living.

There is one addiction that is especially pertinent as we begin the final chapter of this book, and, bearing in mind that it is not particularly new, nor merely some over-hyped creation of the media, it is one that remains strangely unspoken. This 'hidden' addiction can send the sufferer plunging from elation to despair and back up again with the emotional turbulence of a manic depressive. Relatives, friends and colleagues can feel shut out and utterly helpless in preventing the addict seeking ever greater and longer-lasting fixes; indeed, it seems astonishing that there is not a helpline in existence to enable these long-suffering folk to offload their feelings about having to live with what is arguably the most insidious addiction of them all.

## On training to be a therapist

So, what is it, you ask, that engenders such strength of feeling and is seemingly such an impossible habit to break? The answer, for those who have not already guessed from the context, is training addiction or, to put it another way, cloaking oneself in the seductive mantle of the eternal student. The principal area of appeal is fairly obvious: being part of the student fraternity offers the opportunity to Peter Pan one's way through life, eschewing – perhaps that should be denying – the passage of the years, sheltered from the wearisome demands of life which beset normal mortals outside the hallowed halls of learning in the 'real' world.

In terms of therapy training there are particular benefits to be obtained from being involved in apprenticeships that can be perpetuated for many years. And, with so many different trainings on offer these days, it is possible, if one is single-minded enough, to make the role of therapy student as long-running as Agatha Christie's timeless classic, *The Mousetrap*. There are also, however, significant drawbacks in being forever caught in a timewarp of training and the various activities that go with it, and this chapter endeavours to highlight the minuses as well as the pluses.

The first thing to say in examining eternal student syndrome is that ending a psychotherapy or counselling training involves a loss that can be felt as destabilizing or traumatic in varying degrees. With psychotherapy training that loss will be greater simply because of the length of time involved. Given that for many who go into training, therapy represents a second career and that many students are in their 30s, 40s, or even 50s, training can offer a form of identity to those who are suffering from an identity crisis or an erosion of a sense of self. This may involve a lack of meaning or direction brought on by the passing of time, a general lack of fulfilment in life, or a sense of disillusionment with careers that were initiated many years previously when one's outlook on life and ideals were very different.

The process of training to be a therapist often serves to fill the void that has arisen because of the negative feelings listed above. Indeed a good percentage of students never go on to work in the profession of therapy. Training can function as a cloak behind which it is possible to hide away from the angst and difficulties of one's life at that particular time, and thus push aside or deny the negative feelings that go with it. It is here that the real danger lies, in as much as when the training stops the individual loses the new meaning or identity conferred on him by being a student of therapy and is once again forced to face up to the emotional void that confronted him like a yawning chasm before he began training. With couples, for example, training can often be used unconsciously by the training partner to avoid having to face up

## The bitter-sweet taste of freedom

to difficulties within the relationship. So, just as parents are sometimes forced to face the deficiencies in their relationship when children grow up and leave home, the end of training can highlight areas of discontent in a similar way.

These issues around identity are very much akin to the process involved in working with addictions. In my own work with gambling addicts, many of whom have cross-addictions such as drugs and alcohol, one of the most difficult and frustrating periods can be working with the addict when he or she is beginning to give up gambling. Gambling has usually been a huge, sometimes all-consuming facet of their life, not merely in terms of the time spent on the gambling itself but also the planning and calculations involved in trying to beat the bookmaker or the roulette wheel or whatever the gambling medium happens to be, and also the scheming, deceit and lying that is necessary to conceal the gambling from relatives or friends. To give up gambling entails the loss of this whole frenetic sphere of activity, as well as forfeiting the adrenalin kick or the 'escape' factor which is the pay-off of the gambling itself. This leaves a huge void in the gambler's life which, if it is not filled by something almost equally stimulating, will often lead to a relapse.

Furthermore, gambling gives the individual concerned an identity, which they must forfeit when they quit the addiction. For those suffering from a total lack of a sense of self, together with a deep-seated self-hatred, as many addicts are, even a negative identity, which they are fully aware is doing them harm, can be better than no identity at all. Thus to say 'I am a gambler (or a drug addict or an alcoholic)' can seem attractive, self-enhancing and even glamorous and is not something they will let go of lightly.

In its own way, the ending of therapy training can be just as painful and disconcerting as the withdrawal from any addiction. The trainee, now faced with the loss of their student identity, must confront life without this 'badge of authenticity' or emotional crutch. This means they must not only cope with the old feelings and difficulties that were manifesting themselves before training began but must also deal with new emotions and situations engendered by the personal changes and altered dynamics in their relationships brought about by training (as highlighted in Chapter 2). The need to compensate for this huge loss can sometimes be quite manic, as experienced by one counsellor, Linda Nissim, after she ended several years of training:

> *I felt like screaming . . . 'no one prepared me for this!!!!' After six years in the safe environment of training institutions and much discussion about endings, I was not prepared for the sense of loss which, on reflection, I didn't truly acknowledge until a few months*

137

# On training to be a therapist

*later. My first defensive move was to get away, so two or three days after graduation (I will never forget the date!) I took a three-week, long-distance holiday. I returned to find myself telephoning college to enquire about short courses and within a few days had embarked on a 10-week existential course which left me wanting, not because of it's content or quality but because I just wasn't ready. It was too soon. These acting out defences disguised a deep sense of loss of the course, the institution and, most importantly, the weekly contact with those individuals with whom I had cemented deep friendships and for whom I had great admiration, who had been with me on our mutual struggle. Yes, they would still be there for me but everything seemed different now and coming to terms with that difference and embarking on the more lonely pursuit of professional life in this field of work was overwhelmingly painful.*

The loss or the dilution of friendships made on training courses can be especially difficult because given the personal nature of the work and the fact that openness and expression of emotions is an integral part of the process, students often find themselves connecting deeply with 'kindred spirits', leading to meaningful relationships of the kind that are rarely made in the outside world. Yet friendships are by no means the only personal losses that are incurred when training ends. Trainees must also sever connections with tutors and supervisors with whom they may have developed special relationships, and whilst it is possible to retain something of those relationships after the course has ended, as with friendships formed, it can rarely be quite the same afterwards.

This is not merely because of the loss of regular contact, it also has something to do with the course itself, that is the environment and what is created within the structure of the time spent at the training institute. In other words, it is very often the process of training itself that imbues relationships with their meaning, so when the course ends, some or perhaps all of that meaning can wither and die. Some of us will keep some of those friendships and relationships going, more or less undiluted, as I was lucky enough to be able to do, but it is as well to be aware that we can never quite recreate the training situation, nor should we try. Even though certain experiences during training can be special and meaningful, we have to be careful not to idealize them in a way that results in the denigration of other experiences. I did exactly that when my first training course ended and I found myself judging and 'downgrading' my subsequent training and the people on it in the light of the unique and wonderful experience and friendships I had formed on the first course.

## The bitter-sweet taste of freedom

Being separated from the training institute itself can be another form of loss. Our therapeutic alma mater can become a second home both in terms of the people with whom we form connections and also the physical surroundings. That is to say, the rooms, the offices, the gardens, the canteen, etc., can all become a valued and special part of our world. However, the institute and the training course can offer a cocoon from the real world, and just as therapy should not become a substitute for life, so training and the training institute should not do so either.

Finishing training can also mean the end, or at least the winding down, of placements and personal therapy for students who have tied all these elements closely together (others will choose to continue either or both). This also represents a huge loss in terms of meaning and personal relationships. Taking a different perspective, Lesley Murdin (2000: 166) points out a potential danger in ending personal therapy at the same time as ending training:

> . . . some trainees may have been in therapy for many years and have reached a natural stopping place before the end of a long training, and might benefit from experiencing an ending. Those who are able to stop therapy very precipitously at the end of training raise some questions about the value of what they have been doing before, although there may be practical reasons to end soon.

It will often be the case that a placement is linked to training in terms of the length of time involved, which means there is another huge loss, that of ending with clients, to be faced, if not immediately then soon afterwards. Because of limitations on space, it was not possible to devote a section to every possible training issue, and I have chosen not to look at the matter of endings with clients in any detail. Suffice it to say in this context that the process of ending training with all its attendant losses, frequently necessitates a grieving process that has to be acknowledged and worked through. So, if endings with clients are allied to the various other losses which are having to be dealt with on termination of training, this can raise many difficult and painful feelings for trainees.

Murdin (2000: 139) talks of the bereavement process involved in ending therapy, but I believe her observations are also applicable to the end of training:

> Because so much of the work that is done in therapy relates to losses and the way that we face them, the ending phase provides an opportunity that most people find in no other context to live through an ending that has all the measures of sadness, anger,

**139**

# On training to be a therapist

*disappointment, gratitude that go with bereavement and loss in other contexts. These emotions should have been faced before the end, and at the last minute they may be fleeting and easily missed because, if the therapy has gone well, the ending will be a celebration as well as being as loss.*

The celebration aspect which Murdin alludes to can be equated to a memorial service where relatives and friends pay tribute and give thanks for the life of the deceased person. Thus it is possible to feel gratitude, as I did on ending my first training, that I had been part of such a good experience, both in terms of the training itself and the friendships I had formed. However, many trainees are far too preoccupied with anxiety about the aforementioned personal difficulties raised by the ending, as well as professional concerns, such as how they will find work within the profession, to crack open the bubbly. This is why trainees often feel they cannot or will not face up to the end of training and attempt to keep it going in various forms for as long as possible.

For the purposes of this book, I interviewed Shula Wilson, a tutor and supervisor, who is also the clinical director of Skylark, an organization that provides psychotherapy and counselling for people affected by disability. Wilson has a particular interest in the status of being a trainee and the ramifications of ending training. She highlights what is perhaps the most obvious attraction of being the eternal student from a professional perspective: the fact that the we do not have ultimate responsibility for our clients, in other words the buck does not stop with us. In placements and honorary positions we are taken on with full acceptance of our L-plate status, ministered to by supervisors who are, in most cases, mindful of and sympathetic to our limited experience, and in some cases we are given only 'hand-picked' clients who, it is assumed, will not prove to be too troublesome for us to cope with.

Following on from this, there is the thought-provoking question of whether, as trainees, we might feel it is more acceptable for us to make mistakes or to be less 'professional', in contrast to when we are qualified and we take on 'adult' status and more is expected of us. In theory, the idea that we are being indulged to a certain extent because of our trainee tag could be seen as a licence to operate below the levels of competence expected of qualified practitioners. Yet, if we examine that notion it is surely a dangerous, and in most cases patronizing, way of thinking – even if we accept that people train to be therapists for various reasons, not all of them altruistic (as highlighted in Chapter 2).

Because there is a feeling that a safety net exists, there may possibly be a certain degree of unconscious relaxation in terms of not being expected to have all the answers, and also knowing that supervisors and tutors are there to 'mop up' any therapeutic detritus that arises as a result of our inexperience. However, I believe it is reasonable to state that most students of psychotherapy or counselling would never consciously allow themselves to put anything less than 100 per cent into the therapeutic relationship in terms of respect and care for their clients. Of course there are those who will abuse the situation, but they are very much in the minority and the more serious cases will hopefully be 'weeded out' and either apprised of their shortcomings or made to discontinue training.

In this context, it is relevant to consider the issue of exactly what it means to make a mistake, and indeed, what constitutes a mistake in therapeutic terms (see Chapter 6). This in turn brings up the matter of what it means to be seen by others, and to see ourselves, as less than competent. As a positive, self-affirming correlation to this, and without in any way wishing to encourage complacency, I believe it is possible and even desirable to consider a fundamental question: even when we consider ourselves merely humble trainees – and I am including here our earliest fumbling forays with clients – or are recently qualified and sporting the therapeutic version of the green 'P' plates carried by newly qualified drivers, who is to say that the work we do is not at least as therapeutically beneficial as that done by those with vast experience and an array of letters after their names?

Practical reality demands that we do have certain qualifications (although there are plenty of therapists working without any) and this is becoming more and more important as statutory regulation looms, and also as the public become more aware of what to look for when choosing a therapist. However, in terms of our own self-image and the way we feel when we are in sessions with patients, it is arguably not so much about having that piece of paper in our hand, or making what we might perceive as technical errors, but more about how we feel about ourselves internally. Gathering a hatful of diplomas, degrees and doctorates is all very well, but if we are just envisaging them as a kind of mental armour to bolster our self-image it may be worth looking at where our real need lies and spending more time on our own therapist's couch and less in the college.

In terms of feeling qualified internally to do the work, the idea of letting go seems important. Getting to a point where we feel we no longer need training can be said to involve relinquishing the need for nourishment, or if you take a familial image, it is akin to a teenager feeling ready to leave home. (In this context I am not including ongoing professional development, which is desirable – and mandatory for membership of some professional bodies – in terms of our professionalism and our accountability to ourselves, our clients and the profession itself).

## On training to be a therapist

First we have to get to that point where we feel ready to function autonomously without the need for collegial back-up and constant parenting from tutors. Letting go of this need is also very much tied up with fantasies of being the perfect parent ourselves, or, to put it another way, it is a question of whether we can allow ourselves to be less than all-knowing and infallible, and whether we believe that our clients can tolerate a therapist who is less than perfect. Indeed, it could be argued that the notion of perfection is the antithesis of what therapy is about; accepting limitations is very much a part of what we and our clients should be looking towards. Here, once again, Winnicott's ubiquitous notion of 'good enough' comes to mind.

If one puts aside the more pathological, regressive attributes of perpetual training syndrome, it can be said that prolonging student life can be beneficial. It is surely no bad thing to keep the mind active and to learn more and more, both clinically and theoretically, about a profession where even the most experienced and revered practitioners will admit to an endless voyage of discovery. We have to step out alone at some point, however, and, just as children and their parents reach a tacit if frequently fraught understanding of when it is right for them to leave the nest, so we must eventually cut the umbilical ties that bind. Having an internal structure is the key and in this context Erik Erikson (1995: 211–12) provides some appropriate thoughts. Talking about the beginnings of identity, Erikson writes:

> The internalization of . . . 'one who can walk' is one of the many steps in child development which . . . contribute on each step to a more realistic self-esteem. This self-esteem grows to be a conviction that one is learning effective steps towards a tangible future, and is developing into a defined self within a social reality. The growing child must, at every step, derive a vitalizing sense of actuality from the awareness that his individual way of mastering experience (his ego synthesis) is a successful variant of a group identity and is in accord with its space-time and life plan.

The good news amidst all of this apparent negativity is that there *is* life after training – and a potentially enriching and fulfilling life, too. For a start, the enormous practical pressures of training suddenly melt away as if by magic. The curtain falls on the whole manic round of lectures, essay writing, placements, supervision, personal therapy and much more (some of these may be phased out gradually), all of it often part of a juggling act between training, work and family. To quote the golfer, Walter Hagen, we can take time to smell the roses along the way again. Furthermore, psychotherapy and counselling trainings are usually

142

expensive and therefore the very common stress factor of money is also no longer an issue.

In contrast to worries about whether we are ready to work without the support structure of college and placements, there can be a feeling of enormous freedom at the opportunity to be autonomous after all those years of being observed, dissected, restricted and inhibited. A conscientious therapist will arguably never consider himself totally autonomous because of the issue of accountability to one's professional body, and ongoing supervision, which is a requirement for certain organizations such as the British Association for Counselling and Psychotherapy. However, the opportunity to work without having to make detailed process reports of sessions or verbatims, and not to worry about whether one's case study or essay will be up to scratch can feel extremely liberating and can remove inhibitions that may possibly blight our individuality and creativity as therapists.

Furthermore, we can delve as deeply as we like into the reasons why having a piece of paper that says we have passed the course or are registered or accredited with a professional body should not make a difference in terms of how we feel about ourselves professionally, but the fact is that there is something intensely satisfying and validating about completing the course, receiving the documentation and feeling as if we have 'arrived' as a therapist. There is nothing pathological about this, it is simply human to take pride in one's achievements and to feel that all the studying, the clinical endeavour and the long hours have meant something and that they entitle us to be regarded as a recognized and 'adult' practitioner.

It is, of course, natural to feel a little wobbly when faced with the great void that appears to lie ahead, although some will not feel like this, having planned meticulously for the ending by restructuring their lives in various ways or even obtaining client work before their training finishes. As well as issues of loss, there may also be anxiety around finding employment, especially nowadays when there are thousands of people training to be psychotherapists and counsellors every year and therefore an ever greater degree of competition for jobs. I remember one of our tutors telling us around the turn of the new millennium that she had heard of one counselling job advertised in *The Guardian* newspaper for which they had received 300 calls by 11.00 am on the morning the advertisement appeared.

I also recall, at the graduation ceremony for my first diploma, listening with amazement and disbelief as a renowned author and therapist made a thoroughly gloomy speech in her guise as guest of honour, in which she more or less told the assembled throng of students not to bother seeking work in the profession because it was too competitive. Perhaps that should not have come as a surprise from someone whose principal sphere of activity is depression.

The fact that there is fierce competition out there is undeniable, but, because of an increasing – if slightly hesitant – acceptance of the benefits of therapy in global terms, there are also plenty of jobs to be found in an ever-increasing sphere of therapeutic activity. Before looking at how to maximize the chances of getting work, it is necessary to return again to the fundamental question of deciding whether we really want to work in this field (see Chapter 3). I believe many people who enrol on psychotherapy or counselling training courses are doing so because they like the idea of moving into a helping profession or a caring environment and are there to 'get a feel' of the therapeutic world. They may also be attracted because of the possibility of meeting like-minded people in an educational setting.

Whether they are seriously intent on working professionally as a therapist is a different matter. Some will do so full-time, and some will devote part of their life to therapy, possibly mixing it with another career, or they may merely 'dabble' in it, whilst others will go off into the sunset with their qualification and maybe never get around to working professionally within the field. What must be underlined is the need, both during training and on qualification, for a genuine exercise in soul searching combined with a more practical evaluation of what being a therapist involves in terms of personal and emotional commitment (see Chapters 2 and 3) .

The desirability of this type of self-questioning is underlined by Abrahao Brafman (1999: 21):

> *You will find that being a therapist represents a heavy burden and it can often be a painful occupation. If it is true that it may bring you better remuneration than some other occupations, it certainly will never make you rich. It is said that a training analysis is really meant to help you discover why you want to be an analyst: this is a fundamental question you should attempt to answer before you decide to adopt psychotherapy as your career.*

Later, talking of the many people in the helping professions who join psychotherapy training courses to gain experience, Brafman continues (1999: 21):

> *A large proportion of these professionals are exploring 'how it feels' to be with a patient in a psychotherapeutic endeavour. As you well know, not all trainees go on to become full-time or even part-time psychotherapists and I would urge you to suspend this decision for a time, if at all possible.*

# The bitter-sweet taste of freedom

If the result of the self-questioning is a decisive 'yes', then it is necessary to face up to the thorny question of how to find work. From personal experience and the experience of colleagues, not just in the world of therapy but in the larger context of employment generally, the first thing I would suggest is not to place too much reliance on advertisements in newspapers and journals. This is because, as my story about the advertisement in *The Guardian* exemplified, these publicly-advertised positions are usually swamped by applicants and you will therefore be facing vast competition. I am not suggesting one should ignore these advertisements altogether, far from it. I have known more than one fellow trainee who obtained a very good and well-paid position through such an advertisement, in the face of enormous competition, and I have no doubt that many others have done likewise.

The point I am making is that instead of being relatively passive and restricting oneself to advertised positions, in other words waiting for the work to appear, the strategy should be more attacking. To explain this, my father always said that he put his great success in business principally down to two things. The first was to turn a deaf ear to those who say such things as 'There's no work to be had in that particular area, or at this particular time because of the recession, or Christmas, or whatever'. The second, when looking to secure new business, was to target every possible area by firing off as many letters as was humanly possible. My father said that if he received one 'yes' from a thousand letters the exercise had been worthwhile.

Using those tactics as a basis for seeking work as a therapist, I suggest writing to every possible source of work, whether it be hospitals, educational establishments, businesses or any other possible area of employment, detailing your background and attaching a curriculum vitae. As with so many things in life, timing is of the essence, but the good thing about writing unsolicited letters, as opposed to responding to an advertisement, is that if your letter just happens to drop on someone's desk at the right moment and generates a spark of interest, you will not be in competition with anyone else.

There are other ways of finding employment, most of which involve immersing oneself in the world of therapy on a continuing basis. Ongoing training, or continuing professional development (CPD), as it is now called, is not merely a means of maintaining one's professional growth after training has ended. Attending lectures, workshops and seminars, etc., is also a good way of making new contacts and networking, which is at least half the battle when it comes to finding work in the world of therapy.

As an adjunct to ongoing training, there are many benefits to be obtained from peer group supervision, one of which is the potential

## On training to be a therapist

for securing work. Discussing problems and issues with people you have trained with and get on well with can be both edifying and enjoyable – though from personal experience it is all too easy for the fun side to take over and for supervision sessions to degenerate into purely social events. For those working in private practice there is considerable potential benefit to be gained from staying in touch with fellow trainees because as they develop their own practices there can be referrals from one to another. Colleagues may also apprise us of jobs they hear of from their own sources which, for whatever reason, they are not interested in taking themselves.

Earlier I talked of the desirability of 'immersing oneself in the world of therapy' in order to find work, but this phrase should also sound a warning note. As highlighted in Chapter 3, there is a real danger in working as a therapist of giving so much of ourselves to clients that we lose sight of and relinquish our own needs. Consequently we can almost cease to exist as a people in our own right. In this context, the words of Soren Kierkegaard in *The Sickness Unto Death* (1989: 1) make salutary reading: 'The biggest danger, that of losing oneself, can pass off in the world as quietly as if it were nothing; every other loss, an arm, a leg, five dollars, a wife, etc., is bound to be noticed.'

In order to avoid this insidious loss of self, it is essential to put certain parameters around our professional life and maintain them rigidly. We should seek to build in other facets to our existence that take us right away from therapy and everything to do with it. This can include mixing with people from different walks of life on a regular basis and having a circle of friends who have no connection with the world of therapy (it must be stressed that there is nothing wrong with having friends who *are* therapists, too).

Anthony Storr (1995: 188) covers this point:

> *Another danger for the therapist is that of being cut off from contact with ordinary people. Some analysts are quite unable to communicate with anyone other than patients and other analysts. These are the analysts who spend eight hours or more per day seeing patients and then, when evening comes, dutifully attend an analytic seminar. Such a life diminishes one as a human being ... I think it very important that therapists have as normal a social life as possible, in which they meet as friends people in entirely different walks of life who pursue entirely different vocations.*

It is also beneficial to read books that have no therapeutic content, including novels that offer pure enjoyment as well as those that provide enlightenment or edification; to go to the cinema, concerts, shows, etc. and indulge in 'normal' activities such as spending time with partners and children in a way that offers a genuine release from the emotional pressure that can so easily build up. Perhaps most important of all, though, we must cultivate two of our most vital senses – a sense of perspective and a sense of humour. Without those two we risk being diminished as human beings that much faster.

When we have just qualified and are setting out to work in the profession 'for real', it is only natural, and indeed desirable, to put heart and soul into our new vocation and, in attempting to build up our careers, to grasp every piece of work that comes our way. But having a quality of life that offers variety and spiritual and emotional nourishment is not merely a safeguard against burn-out. It will ultimately make us better therapists, less tunnel-visioned and more able to draw on and bring into the therapeutic encounter different aspects of life and more broadly-based experiences that can only serve to enrich our understanding of our clients.

Talking of endings in therapy, Murdin writes (2000: 140):

> *Birth is a difficult process for the baby, as we all know, but recent thinking implies that the baby may actually be ready to be born. The womb may have become a cramped space. The analogy with therapy is obvious and optimistic. We cannot, however, ignore the analogy with the other end of the life span. Jung emphasised that achieving readiness to die is one of the tasks of adult life.*

Murdin's remarks seem apposite for the termination of training, too. As we arrive at the end of the long and winding road our task is to feel ready to allow our 'old' life of training to pass away and to take on the mantle of our new life with full acceptance of everything it entails. There may be feelings of loss, fear and emptiness for some, but there can also be anticipation, excitement, joy and even euphoria. My supervisor in my work with gambling addiction always says that it is important to 'stroke' clients, that is to praise and encourage them, when they report a significant achievement, such as resisting a serious temptation to gamble or being gambling-free for a long period.

So, if you are about to qualify or have recently done so, take time to stroke yourself – you have survived, you have arrived, you have accomplished something very special. You have reached journey's end – yet in one sense it is merely the beginning.

# References

Badcock, C. (1993) *Essential Freud*. Oxford: Blackwell.

Bentall, R.P. (1992) A proposal to classify happiness as a psychiatric disorder, *Journal of Medical Ethics*, 18: 94–8.

Bion, W.R. (1974) *Brazilian Lectures 1*. Rio de Janeiro: Imago Editora.

Bion, W.R. (1996) *Experiences in Groups*. London: Routledge.

Bowlby, J. (1991) *Attachment, Separation and Loss*, 3 vols. London: Penguin.

Brafman, A. (1999) Letter to a young psychotherapy trainee, *The Psychotherapy Review*, 1(1): 16–22.

Brightman, B.K. (1984) Narcissistic issues in the training of the psychotherapist, *International Journal of Psychoanalytic Psychotherapy*, 10: 293–317.

Brown, D. and Pedder, J. (1994) *Introduction to Psychotherapy*. London: Routledge.

Campbell, J. (1988) *The Power of Myth*. New York: Doubleday.

Casement, P. (1995) *On Learning from the Patient*. London: Routledge.

Clarkson, P. (1999) *The Therapeutic Relationship*. London: Whurr.

Coltart, N. (1992) *Slouching Towards Bethlehem*. London: Free Association.

Cushway, D. (1997) Stress in trainee psychotherapists, in V.P. Varma (ed.) *Stress in Psychotherapists*. London: Routledge.

Dale, F. (1997) Stress and the personality of the psychotherapist, in V.P. Varma (ed.) *Stress in Psychotherapists*. London: Routledge.

Dexter, G. (1999) Bad for your health?, *Counselling News*, 15: 1, 3 and 11.

Dryden, W. and Thorne, B. (1991) Approaches to the training of counsellors, in W. Dryden and B. Thorne (eds) *Training and Supervision for Counselling in Action*. London: Sage.

Dryden, W. and Thorne, B. (2000) *Training and Supervision for Counselling in Action*. London: Sage.

Erikson, E.H. (1995) *Childhood and Society*. London: Vintage.

# References

Erwin, E. (1997) *Philosophy and Psychotherapy*. London: Sage.

Freeman, S.C. (1992) C.H. Paterson on client-centred supervision: an interview, *Counselor Education and Supervision*, 31(4): 219–26.

Fromm, E. (1998) *The Art of Listening*. London: Constable.

Gelso, C.J. and Carter, J.A. (1985) The relationship in counseling and psychotherapy: components, consequences and theoretical antecedents, *The Counselling Psychologist*, 13(2): 155–243.

Goldberg, C. (1993) *On Being a Psychotherapist*. New Jersey: Jason Aronson.

Gitelson, M. (1952) The emotional position of the analyst in the psycho-analytic situation, *International Journal of Psycho-analysis*, 33: 1–10.

Heimann, P. (1950) On counter-transference, *International Journal of Psycho-analysis*, 32: 32–40.

Hinshelwood, R.D. (1991) *A Dictionary of Kleinian Thought*. New Jersey: Jason Aronson.

Holmes, C. (1998) *There Is No Such Thing As a Therapist*. London: Karnac.

Horney, K. (1937) *The Neurotic Personality of Our Time*. London: W.W. Norton.

Howe, D. (1993) *On Being a Client: Understanding the Process of Counselling and Psychotherapy*. London: Sage.

Jacobs, M. (1994) Supervising pairs. Private communication for supervision course (part two), Leicester University.

Jacobs, M. (1995a) *D.W. Winnicott*. London: Sage.

Jacobs, M. (1995b) *The Presenting Past*. Buckingham: Open University Press.

Jacobs, M. (1996) *Psychodynamic Counselling in Action*. London: Sage.

Jaques, E. (1965) Death and the mid-life crisis, *International Journal of Psychoanalysis*, 46: 502–13.

Jones, E. (1951) The God Complex. *Essays in Applied Psychoanalysis, Vol 2*. London: Hogarth Press.

Jung, C.G. (1928) Analytical Psychology and Education, in *Contributions to Educational Psychology*. London: Kegan Paul, Trench, Trubner.

Jung, C.G. (1933) *Modern Man in Search of a Soul*. London: Routledge and Kegan Paul.

Jung, C.G. (1973) *Modern Man in Search of a Soul*. London: Routledge and Kegan Paul.

Kierkegaard, S. (1989) *The Sickness Unto Death*. London: Penguin.

Langs, R. (1979) *The Supervisory Experience*. New York: Jason Aronson.

Langs, R. (1998) *Ground Rules in Psychotherapy and Counselling*. London: Karnac.

Lomas, P. (1987) *The Limits of Interpretation*. London: Constable.

Lomas, P. (1994) *True and False Experience*. New Brunswick: Transaction.

Macaskill, N. and Macaskill, A. (1992) Psychotherapists in training evaluate their personal therapy: results of UK survey, *British Journal of Psychiatry*, 9: 133–8.

Mann, D. (1997) *Psychotherapy: An Erotic Relationship*. London: Routledge.

Masson, J. (1997) *Against Therapy*. London: Harper Collins.

May, R. (1996) *The Meaning of Anxiety*. London: W.W. Norton.

McDougall, J. (1986) *Theatres of the Mind*. London: Free Association.

McLeod, J. (2001) Critical issues in the methodology of qualitative research (Introduction), *Counselling and Psychotherapy Research*, 1(2): 115–17.

# On training to be a therapist

Mearns, D. (2000) On being a supervisor, in W. Dryden and B. Thorne (eds) *Training and Supervision for Counselling in Action*. London: Sage.

Miller, A. (1987) The Drama of Being a Child. London: Virago.

Morris, E. (1996) The love that dare not speak its name, in K. Hunt and M. Robson (eds) *Counselling and Passion*. Durham: School of Education, University of Durham.

Murdin, L. (2000) *How Much Is Enough?* London: Routledge.

Nietzsche, F. (1976) Thus spoke Zarathustra: first part, in *The Portable Nietzsche*. London: Penguin.

Orlinsky, D. and Howard, K.I. (1986) Process and outcome in psychotherapy, in S.L. Garfield and A.E. Bergen (eds) *Handbook of Psychotherapy and Behaviour Change*, 3rd edn. New York: Wiley.

Patton, M.J. and Meara, N.M. (1996) Kohut and Counselling: Applications of self-psychology, *Psychodynamic Counselling*, 2(3): 328–55.

Page, S. and Wosket, V. (1995) *Supervising the Counsellor*. London: Routledge.

Phillips, A. (1999) *The Beast in the Nursery*. London: Faber and Faber.

Plato (1997) The apology, in J.M. Cooper and D.S. Hutchinson (eds) *Plato Complete Works*. Indianapolis/Cambridge: Hackett Publishing.

Pollens, B. (1993) The analyst's role: to interpret or to react? in E. Hammer (ed.) *Use of Interpretation in Treatment*. New Jersey: Jason Aronson.

Reik, T. (1998) *Listening with the Third Ear*. New York. Noonday.

Riviere, J. (1958) A character trait of Freud's, in J.D. Sutherland (ed.) *Psychoanalysis and Contemporary Thought*. London: Hogarth Press and Institute of Psycho-analysis.

Rogers, C.R. (1961) *On Becoming a Person: A Therapist's View of Psychotherapy*. London: Constable.

Rogers, C.R. (1998) *On Becoming a Person*. London: Constable.

Rowan, J. (1992) Response to K. Mair, The myth of therapist expertise, in W. Dryden and C. Feltham (eds) *Psychotherapy and its Discontents*. Buckingham: Open University Press.

Russell, B. (2000) *The Conquest of Happiness*. London: Routledge.

Rycroft, C. (1995) *A Critical Dictionary of Psychoanalysis*. London: Penguin.

Singer, E. (1993) The reluctance to interpret, in E. Hammer (ed.) *Use of Interpretation in Treatment*. New Jersey: Jason Aronson.

Smail, D. (1978) *Psychotherapy: A Personal Approach*. London: J.M. Dent.

Smail, D. (2001) *Why Therapy Doesn't Work*. London: Constable & Robinson.

Spencer, M. (2000) Working with issues of difference in supervision of counselling, *Psychodynamic Counselling*, 6(4): 509–19.

Spinelli, E. (1998) *Demystifying Therapy*. London: Constable.

Spinelli, E. (2001) News from the Academic Dean, *Regent's College School of Psychotherapy and Counselling Newsletter*, Winter: 3–4.

Stern, D.N., Sander, L.W., Nahum, J.P. *et al.* (1998) Non-interpretive mechanisms in psychoanalytic theory, *International Journal of Psychoanalysis*, 79(5): 903–21.

Storr, A. (1991) *The Dynamics of Creation*. London: Penguin.

Storr, A. (1995) *The Art of Psychotherapy*. London: Butterworth-Heinemann.

Strasser, F. (1999) *Emotions*. London: Duckworth.

# References

Strasser, F. and Karter, J. (unpublished) *Seeing the Bigger Picture – New Perspectives on Self-Image.*

Strean, H.S. (1991) *Behind the Couch.* New York: Continuum.

Sussman, M.B. (1992) *A Curious Calling.* New Jersey: Jason Aronson.

Symington, N. (1996) *The Making of a Psychotherapist.* London: Karnac.

Szecsody, I. (1990) Supervision: a didactic or mutative situation, *Psychoanalytic Psychotherapy*, 4(3): 245–61.

Teitlebaum, S.H. (1990) Supertransference: the role of the supervisor's blind spots, *Psychoanalytic Psychology*, 7: 243–58.

Thomas, S. (1997) Supervision as a maturational process, *Psychodynamic Counselling*, 3(1): 63–76.

Thorne, B. (1991) *Person Centred Counselling: Therapeutic and Spiritual Dimensions.* London: Whurr.

UKCP (2000) *Ethical Requirements for Member Organisations.* London: United Kingdom Council for Psychotherapy.

van Deurzen-Smith, E. (1997) *Everyday Mysteries.* London: Routledge.

Williams, D. and Irving, J. (1998) Tower of cards, *Counselling News*, 14: 7 and 9.

Winnicott, D.W. (1960) The theory of the parent-infant relationship, *International Journal of Psychoanalysis*, XLI: 585–95.

Winnicott, D.W. (1996) *Through Paediatrics To Psychoanalysis.* London: Karnac.

Winnicott, D.W. (1999) *Playing and Reality.* London: Routledge.

Wolberg, L. (1988) *The Technique of Psychotherapy.* New York: Grune & Stratton.

Zaro, J.S., Barach, R., Nedelman, D.J. and Dreiblatt, I.S. (1978) *A Guide for Beginning Pychotherapists.* Cambridge: Cambridge University Press.

# Index

# On training to be a therapist

# Index

# On training to be a therapist

# Index

Spinelli, Ernesto
  effectiveness, 75, 76–7, 78
  quality control, 97–8
splitting, 37, 56
Stanley, Joe, 33
Steele, Lisa, 131
Stern, Daniel, 107
Stevenson, Robert Louis, 8, 46
Storr, Anthony
  danger of isolation, 146
  self-abnegation of therapists, 52, 53
  writing, 71–2
Strasser, Freddie, 50, 95
Strean, Herbert, 38–9, 52
stress, 48–9
superego, 15
supervision, 81–95
  countertransference, 91–2
  role of non-presenter, 93–4
  sibling rivalry, 92–3
surviving, reliability, 47–8
Sussman, M.B., 17, 86
Symington, Neville, 58
syntonic countertransference, 92
Szecsody, I., 89–90

Teitlebaum, S.H., 86
theory
  competitiveness of writers, 66–8
  definition, 67
  essay writing, 68–74
  limitations, 65–6
  and practice, 75–9
therapeutic alliance, 99, 106–10
  therapist's failure, 110–13
therapy
  aim of, 58–61
  effectiveness of, 61–4

Thomas, Sandra, 89–90
Thorne, Brian, 32
  ethics, 108–9
  personal therapy, 51
Tower, Shawn, 120
training courses, essay writing, 68–70
'transcendent' syndrome, 18
transference, 53, 56, 123–8
  analyst's, 38
  erotic transference, 128–34

unexamined life, Socrates, 41
United Kingdom Council for Psychotherapy, 6
unknown, need to be open to, 101
unworthiness, feelings of, 21–2

Van Deurzen-Smith, Emmy, 42, 57–8
Von Bertalanffy, Ludwig, 117

Walton, Sandra, 33
Waterman, Jan, 25
Whittam-Smith, Andreas, 6–7, 68
Williams, David, 32
Wilson, Shula, 140
Winnicott, Donald W., 142
  analyst's failure, 110
  false self, 15
  mirroring, 100
  mother–infant relationship, 56–7
  playing and potential space, 4, 90
  survival and reliability, 46
Wolberg, Lewis, 61, 110
working alliance, *see* therapeutic alliance
Wosket, Val, 89, 92
writing, essay writing, 68–74

Zaro, J.S., 85, 102

# openup
ideas and understanding
in social science

# www.**openup**.co.uk

 **Browse, search and
order online**

 **Download detailed
title information and
sample chapters***

*for selected titles

www.**openup**.co.uk

CARDIFF AND VALE COLLEGE

70067651

361·323
KAR

# On training to be a therapist

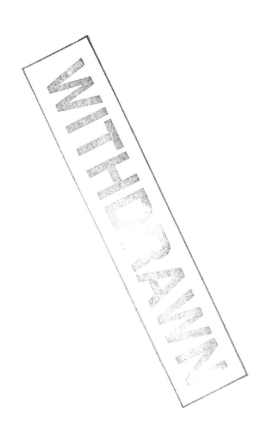

CARDIFF AND VALE COLLEGE